A Framework for Strategy Development

John G. McGinn
Gregory F. Treverton
Jeffrey A. Isaacson
David C. Gompert
M. Elaine Bunn

Prepared for the
Office of the Secretary of Defense

Approved for public release; distribution unlimited

RAND
NATIONAL DEFENSE RESEARCH INSTITUTE

The research described in this report was sponsored by the Office of the Secretary of Defense (OSD). The research was conducted in RAND's National Defense Research Institute, a federally funded research and development center supported by the OSD, the Joint Staff, the unified commands, and the defense agencies under Contract DASW01-01-C-0004.

ISBN: 0-8330-3135-X

RAND is a nonprofit institution that helps improve policy and decisionmaking through research and analysis. RAND® is a registered trademark. RAND's publications do not necessarily reflect the opinions or policies of its research sponsors.

Cover design by Stephen Bloodsworth

Published 2002 by RAND
1700 Main Street, P.O. Box 2138, Santa Monica, CA 90407-2138
1200 South Hayes Street, Arlington, VA 22202-5050
201 North Craig Street, Suite 102, Pittsburgh, PA 15213-1516
RAND URL: http://www.rand.org/
To order RAND documents or to obtain additional information, contact Distribution Services: Telephone: (310) 451-7002;
Fax: (310) 451-6915; Email: order@rand.org

This report contains the results of a study on strategy development, sponsored by the Deputy Assistant Secretary of Defense (Strategy), Office of the Secretary of Defense (OSD). The purpose of the study was to assist the Department of Defense (DoD) in its efforts to refine current defense strategy in light of recent experiences and to address expectations about future challenges to U.S. national security. The principal objective of the study was to develop a new framework that better links military strategy to resource prioritization and making investment choices.

The research for this report was completed prior to the attacks of September 11, 2001, and the publication of the *Quadrennial Defense Review Report* on September 30, 2001. Because the purpose of this report is to document a methodology that served as input to the DoD strategy review and the Quadrennial Defense Review (QDR), it has not been updated in light of the September events.

This report will be of interest to the OSD, the services, defense analysts, and others concerned with the development of national military strategy. The research was conducted within the International Security and Defense Policy Center of RAND's National Defense Research Institute, a federally funded research and development center sponsored by the OSD, the Joint Staff, the unified commands, and the defense agencies.

CONTENTS

FIGURES

TABLES

The U.S. military strategy of "Shape, Respond, Prepare Now" was developed during the course of the 1997 Quadrennial Defense Review. Specifically, this strategy stated that the DoD had an essential role to play in shaping the international security environment, that it must be capable of responding to the full spectrum of crises, and that it needed to be preparing now for an uncertain future.

With slight modifications, this QDR strategy remained the rationale for the employment of U.S. military forces until late 2001.[1] This strategy, as defined more extensively in the *Report of the Quadrennial Defense Review* (Cohen, 1997) and subsequent defense reports, had many virtues: It was defined broadly enough to encompass the spectrum of military operations from peacekeeping and humanitarian assistance through high-intensity warfare, it had a prominent focus on future challenges, and it made explicit the important role of the military in deterring conflict.

On the other hand, as noted by the National Defense Panel (NDP) and others, the strategy was longer on philosophy than it was on practicalities. In particular, the link to resource allocation was rather tenuous, and neither the QDR strategy nor subsequent decisions provided much guidance in framing the key choices for defense. Moreover, despite the stated breadth of the strategy, the United States maintained an overall force posture (including states of readi-

---

[1]The 2001 *QDR Report*, published on September 30, 2001, formally superseded the 1997 strategy. The new strategy of "Assure, Dissuade, Deter, and Decisively Defeat" replaced "Shape, Respond, Prepare Now." The *QDR Report* is available at http://www.defenselink.mil/pubs/qdr2001.pdf.

ness and orientation) that was designed for responding to two near-simultaneous major theater wars (MTWs), rather than the full spectrum of anticipated military missions. This proved untenable, however, because the constant stream of lesser contingencies put a great strain on the force structure, which could not realistically be maintained at high readiness for the stereotypical two-MTW scenario.

In view of the foregoing, this report outlines a preliminary framework designed to better link strategy with resource prioritization and more accurately frame key investment choices on force structure and other elements of the defense program.[2]

A NEW FRAMEWORK FOR DEVELOPING STRATEGY

Strategy development has both objective and subjective aspects, and a key goal of this work is to craft an adaptable framework that accounts for each. The framework (as illustrated in Figure S.1) seeks to lay out the elements of a strategy in a logical and transparent way. It provides a space in which decisionmakers can first display strategic options and their inherent tradeoffs, then debate the merits of these competing choices, and then finally decide on a specific strategy.

A number of steps are involved in crafting the framework. Suppose a decisionmaker wanted to give strategic priority to policing global instability, or to preparing for competition with China, or to another specific challenge. The first step would be elucidating preferences for strategic emphasis. We call these preferences *themes,* and in this report we consider six that cover a broad spectrum of strategic objectives, rationales, and potential contingencies: "Ambitious Shaping," "Countering Rogues," "Protecting the Homeland," "Countering New Dangers," "Preparing for China," and "Policing Instability."[3] The

---

[2] This research was completed prior to the attacks of September 11, 2001, and the publication of the 2001 *QDR Report* on September 30, 2001. Because the purpose of this report is to document a methodology that served to provide input to the DoD strategy review and the QDR, it has not been updated in light of the September events.

[3] Other types of themes could be used in developing a strategic construct. The six themes discussed in this report are merely examples, albeit with real-life applications, that are presented to illustrate the construction and application of the framework. Similarly, the three constructs discussed in this report are examples of potentially many constructs that are created by mixing and matching various themes.

framework then links those themes to the respective force postures (that is, how to best structure, deploy, and position U.S. forces, and how to use those forces for fighting) and special capability packages (for example, those sets of capabilities required to conduct missile defense, information operations, or stability operations) that are necessary to carry out those themes. No single theme on its own amounts to a strategy, but several themes can be combined in different ways to provide the rudimentary foundation of a strategy.

In the next step in creating the framework, we look illustratively at three pairs of themes, labeled "Provisional Constructs" in Figure S.1, which, as the figure shows, reflect different "Approaches" (alternative views of the world and of the U.S. role within it). The framework then provides ways to test these constructs against the drivers of the future security environment; thereby both the relevance and feasibility of the various constructs can be examined. Based on that test, the constructs can then be refined. The refined constructs can then be presented as "Illustrative Portfolios" (as seen in Figure S.1) that suggest where to invest resources, where to divest resources, and where to maintain existing capabilities. Looking across several of the revised portfolios provides an indication of which capabilities are relatively common and which are less necessary, and, especially, what key choices are implied by moving toward one portfolio or another. Herein lies the crucial link between strategy and resources.

ARTICULATING STRATEGIC THEMES

The strategic themes are distinct enough to have specific implications for the defense program and yet cover a wide range of choices about U.S. interests and the future security environment.

Ambitious Shaping

This theme is based on the rationale that a formative moment in the world's political geography is happening right now. The world's core of nation-states—those states that are democracies and have market economies—is strong and growing larger, and much of the globe's political future will turn on whether major *transition states*—chiefly China and Russia, but also India and others—remain on the path toward democracy and economic openness. Thus, the task associated

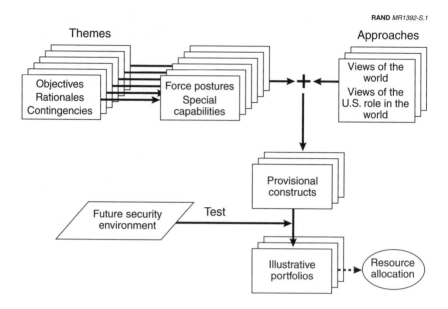

Figure S.1—Framework for Strategy Development

with this theme is twofold: to turn U.S. allies into full partners in shaping the world before us, and, especially, to devote special attention to large transition states (in particular, China and Russia) and what the United States can do to ensure that their transition to pluralistic political systems and market economies will succeed.

The instruments used in this environment shaping may, in fact, be more political and economic instruments than they are military ones. Operationally, this theme emphasizes expeditionary operations to decisively defeat potential adversaries and engagement activities of all sorts targeted on both allies and transition states. This theme seeks to use the U.S. military to build connections with transition states through combined exercises, coalition operations, and military-to-military contacts and exchanges. At the same time, America's ability to shape the future security environment also depends on continued and unquestioned U.S. military strength.

Countering Rogues

This theme is rooted in the premise that rogue states (such as Iraq, Iran, and North Korea) will continue to be a threat to the United States. Rogue states are more or less alienated from the global system and are considered to be dangerous, but their military capabilities are somewhat limited. Because they are militarily weaker than the United States, rogue states may resort to asymmetric measures such as reliance on weapons of mass destruction (WMD) as a threat and, possibly, as a fact of war. More generally, they will seek to exploit the United States' Achilles' heels through anti-access strategies accompanied by short-warning attacks and quick movement into cities, for example.

The objective of this theme is thus to deter and, if required, defeat those rogues. Operationally, it does not necessarily assume that countering rogues will require future Desert Storms. It does imply, however, that greater attention should be paid to countering the threat of WMD attacks and to building combat capabilities that include strong projection forces, forward stationing, and the ability to defeat anti-access strategies.

Protecting the Homeland

This theme focuses on the need for the United States to worry less about the world, which seems to be coming along reasonably well, and be concerned more about itself. The objective of this theme, then, is to elevate the importance of protecting the U.S. territory and its citizens. In embracing this theme, one may or may not believe that the United States should pull back somewhat from its obligations and deployments abroad. The theme is not, in itself, isolationist, but rather an expression of the belief that homeland defense has been shortchanged.

Operationally, this theme focuses on defending against missiles, countering WMD and major non-WMD terrorism, and protecting U.S. and allied information systems. These actions would concentrate on preemption, but also on dealing with the consequences of attacks. This would entail a greater role for the military (especially the Reserves and National Guard) in homeland defense, but also necessitates the ability to conduct expeditionary operations to eliminate threats overseas. This theme would also require a great deal of coordination between the DoD and nonmilitary agencies.

Countering New Dangers

This theme centers on confronting the new and largely unconventional challenges in the global system. Its rationale is that the positive aspects of globalization (for example, free-market capitalism, democratization, and increasing zones of peace and prosperity) will continue as will U.S. military superiority. States that might be potential adversaries of the United States are deterred. The United States thus has both the need and the luxury to focus on unfamiliar threats, with most of them being *transnational*—that is, threats resulting not from the actions of nation-states but rather from the underside of globalization. The objective of this theme is to prevent and, if need be, deter such new threats.

Operationally, this theme would focus on countering WMD terrorism and non-WMD terrorism by non-state actors, the trafficking of illegal drugs, and information warfare. As with the Protecting the Homeland theme, these sorts of activities would require a great deal of coordination between the DoD and nonmilitary agencies.

Preparing for China

This theme centers on preparing for the emergence of a military and economic near peer. The rationale is that, in the long run, of all the transition states only China can pose anything like a peer-level threat to the United States. This does not presume that China will be an enemy, only that China's emerging capabilities will determine the benchmark by which U.S. forces should be judged, and that China's own military growth will be less threatening if it takes place in the recognized shadow of U.S. military superiority.

This theme's objective is to prevent Chinese military ascendancy by making the U.S. military superiority clear and to shape China into a true strategic partner. Operationally, this theme would emphasize the continued capacity to project military power into Asia, interoperability with regional allies, and defense against China's medium- and long-range missiles. It would mean staunch support for friendly regional states such as Japan, Korea, and Taiwan. And it would mean increasing, rather than decreasing, basing options for operations in the Asia-Pacific region. The focus of power projection would likely be on naval and aerospace operations.

Policing Instability

Like the Countering New Dangers theme, the Policing Instability theme addresses the underside of otherwise favorable trends. Motivated by the expectation that the positive aspects of globalization will continue and U.S. strength will continue to deter major state-centered threats, this theme hypothesizes that terrorism (with and without WMD), while being a factor, is muted by global economic growth and U.S. military power. This theme aims to lead coalitions of willing allies to preserve and restore order in those places where "good" globalization fails to take root. It would concentrate on multilateral stability operations and engagement activities of all sorts. This theme reflects much of the recent past when, lacking serious enemies, the United States has had both the capacity and the discretion to decide where and when it would intervene to police instability.

LINKING STRATEGIC THEMES TO FORCE POSTURES AND CAPABILITIES

Although the themes we just described are not truly distinct, they do tend to require different military capabilities. For example, policing instability would require less-conventional combat capability than, say, countering rogues. Similarly, protecting the homeland would require greater emphasis on missile defense than would ambitious shaping. To flesh out these differences, we defined three *force postures* and seven *special capability packages.*[4]

The following three force postures reflect basic choices on how to structure, deploy, and position U.S. forces, and how to use those forces for fighting. They are the basic building blocks of defense.

---

[4]The force postures and capability packages discussed in this report are examples used for illustrative purposes. The framework can be applied to other types of postures and capabilities.

- **Traditionally Configured Combat Forces.** This force posture generally reflects the current disposition of U.S. military forces: division building blocks for ground forces, traditional aircraft and air forces, and carrier-centered naval operations.

- **Expeditionary Forces.** This force posture envisions a greater number of modular and rapidly deployable forces capable of responding to diverse contingencies around the world—brigade building blocks for ground forces, multirole aircraft in a fully implemented Air Expeditionary Force (AEF), and fewer carrier-centered naval operations.

- **Forces-After-Next Focus.** This posture envisions a more radical shift in the nature of military forces and would emphasize leap-ahead technology. The outcome is unclear and alternative concepts may prove out, but what some proponents have in mind are ground and air forces built from smaller-than-brigade/wing-building blocks and naval operations using smaller platforms, such as Streetfighter. The expectation is that there will be a premium placed on dispersal and long reach.

Like force postures, the special capability packages combine weapons, forces, platforms, and missions, but they also combine sets of resources that are necessary to accomplish particular types of operations and missions. If the force postures represent basic choices, then the special capability packages might be thought of as more-specialized capability add-ons. Some specific special capability packages are

- **Stability Operations**

- **Missile Defense**

- **Countering WMD**

- **Countering Transnational Threats** (for example, crime, illegal drugs, or terrorism)

- **Information Operations**

- **Environment Shaping** (for example, combined exercises, military-to-military contacts, or security assistance)

- **Nontraditional Missions** (for example, humanitarian assistance, civil affairs, or disaster relief).

With the postures and capability packages having been defined, the next step in crafting the strategy-development framework is to identify, for each theme, whether a given package is "very important," "important," or "less important" for carrying out that theme (Chapter Three has a further discussion of this ranking). When themes are combined to create strategic constructs, this ranking will provide the basis for determining investment priorities.

FORMING STRATEGIC CONSTRUCTS

American defense strategy plainly turns on how U.S. leaders view the world and the nation's role within it. This philosophical "approach" to defense policy significantly influences U.S. leaders' strategic choices. Strategic themes reflect an emphasis on particular areas of concern, but a policymaker's vantage point needs to be broader than that.

While the themes remain the basic building blocks of a strategic framework, the next step is to use them to create something that resembles a strategy. The result is a *strategic construct.* Such constructs are developed by mixing a bottom-up view of the strategic themes discussed here with a top-down perspective of the various approaches to defining the U.S. role in the world.

Combining the six strategic themes into pairs produced the following three constructs that illustrate distinct ways in which the United States can formulate its defense strategy.

Focus on Key Responsibilities

This construct roughly combines the attributes of the Countering Rogues and Preparing for China themes. It posits that the United States has a distinct position with special historical responsibilities in the new era, and must confront the most demanding current and future security challenges—with friends, if possible, or alone, if necessary. These challenges include dealing with hostile states that have WMD and the means to deliver them; addressing threats to world energy supplies; maintaining peace in regions that are both vital and potentially insecure (for instance, East and Southwest Asia); and managing the emergence of a powerful China. The United States looks to reduce its commitment to lower-end contingencies, such as the Balkans, so that the military can focus on challenges to more-vital interests such as rogue states or China.

U.S. Multilateral Leadership

This construct roughly combines the attributes of the Ambitious Shaping and Policing Instability themes. It posits that the future of major transition states (such as China and Russia) is far from clear; instability remains high, from the Balkans through Africa and from the Middle East to South, Southeast, and Northeast Asia; and high-intensity conflict is unlikely (because of U.S. military superiority), whereas demands for smaller scale contingencies (SSCs) will persist. This construct is not intended to be a substitute for having strong military forces for deterrence, but rather an expression of an emphasis on the United States working with partners rather than taking on global responsibilities by itself.

Protecting an Essential Core

This construct roughly combines the attributes of the Protecting the Homeland and Countering New Dangers themes. Broadly speaking, it posits that international trends are favorable, and U.S. military superiority is sufficient to protect traditional interests (for example, U.S. territory) from traditional threats (for example, foreign military forces). National security is less demanding in traditional ways but more demanding when faced with unfamiliar challenges to the U.S. territory, its citizens, and the functioning of vital global economic systems.

BUILDING PROVISIONAL CONSTRUCTS BY RATING FORCE POSTURES AND CAPABILITY PACKAGES

The next step is to build *provisional constructs* by examining how the different construct approaches compare given the relative importance of the various force postures and special capability packages.

(We refer to these constructs as being "provisional" because they do not account for the impact of the future security environment or fiscal constraints.) By rating each posture and package as "very important," "important," or "less important," we form the provisional constructs (see Table S.1). These three constructs can be refined by examining their potential vulnerabilities, as identified in a review of the future security environment.

TESTING THE CONSTRUCTS AGAINST THE FUTURE SECURITY ENVIRONMENT

Neither point predictions[5] nor scenarios about the future seemed the right way to test our strategic themes; the former are too narrow and the latter are too complicated. Instead, we focused on future *drivers*, or determinants, that will bear on U.S. military operations. The following ten drivers, grouped in three categories (global context, U.S. capacity,[6] and threats to U.S. security) are primarily expressed as positive assumptions.

Global Context

- Positive globalization—an open economy and a growing core—will continue.

- Negative globalization—the flow of "bads"[7]—such as crime, illegal drugs, and weapons—will be limited.

- Transnational trends, such as increased migration or environmental degradation, will not affect military operations or definitions of U.S. security.

---

[5]By "point prediction," we mean a best guess on where "x" will be by "y" period of time. For example, to say that the economy of a particular state will collapse by 2010 is a point prediction.

[6]"Capacity" refers to the ability of the United States to conduct military operations, maintain defense spending, continue to play a key role in world affairs, and perform other such capabilities.

[7]In this report, the word "bads" refers to the negative consequences of globalization, such as the flow of illegal drugs and weapons. Conversely, "goods" refers to the positive aspects of globalization, such as opportunities for economic growth and increased cooperation among the core industrial nations.

Table S.1

Posture and Capability Ratings for Each Provisional Construct

	Focus on Key Responsibilities	U.S. Multilateral Leadership	Protecting an Essential Core
Force Postures			
Traditionally Configured Combat Forces	Important	Important	Less Important
Expeditionary Forces	Very Important	Very Important	Very Important
Forces-After-Next Focus	Very Important	Less Important	Very Important
Special Capability Packages			
Stability Operations	Important	Very Important	Less Important
Missile Defense	Very Important	Less Important	Very Important
Countering WMD	Very Important	Important	Very Important
Countering Transnational Threats	Important	Important	Very Important
Information Operations	Very Important	Very Important	Very Important
Environment Shaping	Very Important	Very Important	Important
Nontraditional Missions	Less Important	Very Important	Less Important

U.S. Capacity

- The United States will remain rich and technologically advantaged.

- The United States will have domestic support for considerable defense spending.

- The United States will have domestic support for substantial engagement.

- The United States will have rich and strong allies.

Threats to U.S. Security

- Large states, such as Russia, India, and especially China, will make successful transitions toward pluralistic political systems and market economies.

- Attacks on U.S. and allied information systems and WMD attacks will remain isolated or will be contained. States may fail, but the impact of their failure will remain localized.

VULNERABILITIES OF ASSUMPTIONS

In this examination of future drivers, it is more analytically satisfying to work at the building-block level with the strategic themes than at the more-aggregated level of constructs. Because single themes have a sharper emphasis than constructs that encompass more than one theme, they reflect distinct biases about the future. Ambitious shaping, for example, is boldly optimistic, whereas countering rogues, on the other hand, is more profoundly pessimistic. For each strategic theme, we asked the following questions:

- What assumptions does the theme imply about each driver?

- How important is each assumption?

- Which assumptions are most vulnerable to *not* turning out as stated?

Across the themes, it was striking that the assumptions that were more vulnerable to being proved incorrect were clustered within four of the determinants, or drivers, we listed earlier—domestic support for engagement, support by allies, the fate of transition states, and the prospect for attacks on information systems and WMD attacks.

REFINING THE CONSTRUCTS

The last stage in building the strategic framework is refining the three provisional constructs in light of the vulnerabilities identified in the future security environment analysis. This refinement will turn the provisional constructs into *illustrative portfolios* of decisionmaking options that imply resource choices (see Chapter Six for further information on this process).

A principal step in this transition from provisional constructs to illustrative portfolios is to identify possible hedges for each construct based on the constructs' respective vulnerabilities noted in the future security environment analysis. For example, The Nontraditional Missions special capability package is ranked "less important" for the Focus on Key Responsibilities provisional construct because the construct emphasizes preparation for major conflict. This "less important" rating implies that policymakers should possibly "divest" this capability package. However, given the vulnerability of the Focus on Key Responsibilities construct to the possibility that major transition states may become adversaries or that allies may not pick up lesser defense tasks without U.S. participation, a decisionmaker may or may not "hedge" against this vulnerability by raising the ranking of Nontraditional Missions to "maintain." Possible hedges for all of the constructs can be identified in a similar manner.

Table S.2 summarizes the refined portfolios, and also indicates a few hedges that are possible, but not necessary, refinements to the constructs.

APPLYING THE FRAMEWORK

Ultimately, the framework can help decisionmakers prioritize their various needs. The major tradeoffs associated with choosing among the three constructs become more vivid when portrayed graphically, as in Figure S.2.

As shown in the figure, the core forces and capabilities are those force postures and special capability packages that all three portfolios will either invest in or will maintain. Thus, they form a nucleus of key attributes that are important to decisionmakers, regardless of the chosen defense strategy. The key decisions and tradeoffs are those that entail expanding from the core to encompass one or another illustrative portfolio. Moving toward the Protecting an Essential Core portfolio, for example, makes the Forces-After-Next Focus posture the top priority and suggests divesting capacity for traditionally configured forces and nontraditional missions. Moving toward the U.S. Multilateral Leadership portfolio reverses those priorities.

Table S.2

Illustrative Portfolios of Key Decisionmaking Options

	Focus on Key Responsibilities	U.S. Multilateral Leadership	Protecting an Essential Core
Force Postures			
Traditionally Configured Combat Forces	Maintain	Maintain	Divest
Expeditionary Forces	Invest	Invest	Invest
Forces-After-Next Focus	Invest	Maintain[a]	Invest
Special Capability Packages			
Stability Operations	Maintain	Invest	Maintain[a]
Missile Defense	Invest	Maintain[a]	Invest
Countering WMD	Invest	Maintain	Invest
Countering Transnational Threats	Maintain	Maintain	Invest
Information Operations	Invest	Invest	Invest
Environment Shaping	Invest	Invest	Maintain
Nontraditional Missions	Divest	Invest	Divest

[a]Hedged strategic choices modified in response to identified vulnerabilities in the future security environment.

There is also significant room for differentiation within the core forces and capabilities. Although the core covers two of the three force postures and six of the seven special capability packages, there are differences of "invest" versus "maintain" among the three portfolios. So although the three portfolios will have these postures and packages in common, there will be potentially significant differences in emphasis within this core set. Moreover, while these three portfolios happen to have a relatively high degree of complementarity, other constructs might imply a different and less broad set of common postures and capabilities.

The framework is readily adaptable for building other strategies. Different themes can be articulated, and themes can be mixed and matched to build constructs that are different from those shown

RAND *MR1392-S.2*

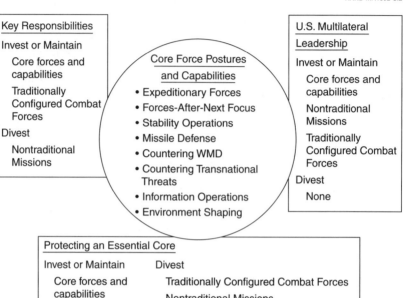

Figure S.2—Identifying Strategic Choices for Three Constructs

here. A change in assessments of the future security environment could also lead to different strategic choices.

Spelling out force postures and capability packages gives clarity to the inherent—but not always readily visible—resource implications of strategic choices and tradeoffs. In that sense, the framework provides a mechanism for connecting the defense strategy to programmatic choices and debating the pros and cons of those choices.

ACKNOWLEDGMENTS

This study was conducted as an unusually collaborative effort with the sponsor, Deputy Assistant Secretary of Defense (Strategy) Andrew Hoehn, and his office (Principal Deputy Barry Pavel and others). The study included numerous roundtable dialogues and briefings that were designed to spark discussion and provide real-time feedback. Numerous RAND colleagues and consultants also made significant contributions to this project. Lowell Schwartz contributed to the budgetary work with some timely assistance. Christopher Layne and Christopher Speckhard conducted exploratory analysis for our future security environment task. Stuart Johnson, Leslie Lewis, Roger Brown, and John Schrader provided valuable feedback and suggestions on improving the framework. Paul Davis validated early parts of the work that became capability packages and provided a rigorous and helpful review. Paul Bracken also provided a very thoughtful and useful review. Finally, Sandy Hanson, Laura Mosser, Tamika Jones, Katy Rees, and Lisa Rogers all contributed valuable administrative assistance, and our thanks to Nancy DelFavero for editing the final report.

ACRONYMS

AEF	Aerospace Expeditionary Force
CBO	Congressional Budget Office
CIP	Critical infrastructure protection
CVBG	Carrier battle group
DoD	Department of Defense
FID	Foreign internal defense
HUMINT	Human intelligence
IA	Information assurance
MTW	Major theater war
NATO	North Atlantic Treaty Organization
NDP	National Defense Panel
NMD	National missile defense
O&M	Operation and maintenance
OSD	Office of the Secretary of Defense
PPBS	Planning, Programming, and Budgeting System
PSYOPS	Psychological operations
QDR	Quadrennial Defense Review

RMA	Revolution in Military Affairs
R&D	Research and development
RTD&E	Research, Test, Development, and Evaluation
SSC	Small-scale contingency
TMD	Theater missile defense
USJFCOM	United States Joint Forces Command
WMD	Weapons of mass destruction

Chapter One

INTRODUCTION

The U.S. military strategy of "Shape, Respond, Prepare Now" was developed during the course of the 1997 Quadrennial Defense Review (QDR). Specifically, this strategy stated that the Department of Defense (DoD) had an essential role to play in shaping the international security environment, that it must be capable of responding to the full spectrum of crises, and that it needed to be preparing now for an uncertain future (Cohen, 1997). With slight modifications, this QDR strategy remained the rationale for the employment of U.S. military forces until late 2001.[1]

The strategy—as defined more extensively in the QDR and in subsequent defense reports[2]—had many virtues: It was defined broadly enough to encompass the spectrum of military operations from peacekeeping and humanitarian assistance through high-intensity warfare, it had a prominent focus on future challenges, and it made explicit the important role of the military in deterring conflict. On the other hand, as noted by the National Defense Panel (NDP)[3] and oth-

---

[1]The 2001 *Quadrennial Defense Review Report,* published on September 30, 2001, formally superseded the 1997 strategy. The new strategy of "Assure, Dissuade, Deter, and Decisively Defeat" replaced "Shape, Respond, Prepare Now." The *QDR Report* is available at http://www.defenselink.mil/pubs/qdr2001.pdf.

[2] For the 2000 defense strategy, see Cohen (2001).

[3]The NDP, an external panel of defense analysts and retired general officers, was established by Congress to critique the QDR and to provide analysis on the long-term issues facing defense and national security. The NDP final report, *Transforming Defense: National Security in the 21st Century* (1997), is at http://www.dtic.mil/ndp. For an in-depth discussion of the NDP, its relationship to the QDR, and an analysis of the final report and its impact, see Tedstrom and McGinn (1999).

ers, the Shape, Respond, Prepare Now strategy was longer on philosophy than it was on practicalities.

Although some research that was central to the first QDR used a portfolio-management approach,[4] little connection between high strategy and the normal DoD Planning, Programming, and Budgeting System (PPBS) ensued. In particular, the link to resource allocation was rather tenuous, and neither the strategy as defined in the QDR nor subsequent decisions provided much guidance in framing the key choices for defense.[5]

Moreover, despite the stated breadth of the strategy, the United States maintained an overall force posture (including states of readiness and orientation) that was designed for responding to two major theater wars (MTWs), rather than the full spectrum of anticipated military missions.[6] This proved untenable, however, because the constant stream of lesser contingencies put great strain on the force structure, which could not realistically be maintained at high readiness for the stereotypical two-MTW scenario.

In view of the foregoing, this report outlines a preliminary framework to better link strategy to resource prioritization and to frame key investment choices on force structure and other elements of the defense program.[7]

TRENDS IN DEFENSE SPENDING

The first task in this study was to test the connection between strategy and resources. Do they in fact connect? The short answer is no. The disconnects between the current strategy and the defense budget become clearer as one examines trends in defense spending over the past decade. U.S. defense spending has declined significantly

---

[4]See especially Davis et al. (1996).

[5]Some research did attempt to lay out ways to root military transformation into strategic objectives. See, for example, Davis et al. (1998).

[6]For discussions on this issue, see Gompert and Lachow (2000) and Davis (1994).

[7]This research was completed prior to the attacks of September 11, 2001, and the publication of the 2001 *QDR Report* on September 30, 2001. Because the purpose of this report is to document a methodology that served as input to the DoD strategy review and the QDR, it has not been updated in light of the September events.

since the end of the Cold War. This reduction of budget authority (in billions of year-2000 dollars) is illustrated in Table 1.1 (U.S. Congressional Budget Office, 2000).

This reduction in spending has been coupled with a concomitant reduction in DoD personnel and force structure. Since 1989, for example, the number of active-duty military personnel has dropped 35 percent to 1.39 million soldiers. Conventional force structure has also been greatly reduced during this same time. Some of the major force reductions are illustrated in Table 1.2 (U.S. Congressional Budget Office, 2000).

These significant reductions in defense spending and force structure have not, however, been accompanied by reduced employment of American soldiers around the world. To the contrary, since the end of the Persian Gulf War in 1991, U.S. military forces have been involved in more than 50 contingency operations abroad, ranging from no-fly-zone operations over Iraq to peace enforcement operations in the Balkans (U.S. General Accounting Office, 2000). While these challenges have generally been different from those faced during the

Table 1.1

Funding for National Defense in Selected Years, 1989 to 1999
(in billions of year-2000 dollars)

	1989	1993	1997	1999	Percentage Change, 1989–1999
Department of Defense					
Military personnel	109	93	78	73	−33
Operations and maintenance	116	99	99	109	−6
Procurement	97	58	44	52	−47
Research, development, test, and evaluation	47	42	38	39	−17
Military construction	7	5	6	6	−20
Family housing	4	4	4	4	−11
Other agencies (Department of Energy and others)	11	16	13	14	23
Total national defense funding	391	318	282	296	−24

Table 1.2

U.S. Military Forces in Selected Years, 1989 to 1999
(in number of major components)

	1989	1993	1997	1999	Percentage Change, 1989–1999
Land Forces					
Army Divisions					
Active	18	14	10	10	–44
Reserve	10	8	8	8	–20
Marine Expeditionary Forces					
Active	3	3	3	3	0
Reserve	1	1	1	1	0
Naval Forces					
Battle Force Ships	566	435	354	317	–44
Aircraft carriers					
Active	15	13	11	11	–27
Reserve	1	0	1	1	0
Air wings					
Active	13	11	10	10	–23
Reserve	2	2	1	1	–50
Air Forces					
Fighter wings					
Active	25	16	13	13	–48
Reserve	12	11	8	8	–33
Airlift aircraft					
Intertheater	401	382	345	331	–17
Intratheater	468	380	430	425	–9

Cold War, the principal force structure elements have not changed. There are fewer Army divisions, Navy aircraft carriers, and Air Force wings today than there were in 1989, but those organizations remain the major building blocks for military operations today.

THE STRATEGY-RESOURCE DISCONNECT

The increased number of military operations conducted by a substantially smaller military have led to strains on both military readiness and defense budgets. Defense analysts have alternatively contended that the U.S. military is overworked,[8] underfunded,[9] improperly structured for today's challenges,[10] or some combination of these factors.[11] What is clear, however, is that there is a significant disconnect between what U.S. forces are doing to implement the defense strategy and what they are resourced to do. Some believe that the total level of funding is inadequate, but many believe that procurement is severely underfunded.

This mismatch between strategy and resources has received much attention in the defense community recently.[12] Much of this attention has centered on the particularly stark deficits in the Procurement budgetary account. Dramatic shortfalls over the next several years between planned appropriations and planned purchases of weapons systems, such as the F-22 Raptor fighter, the Crusader artillery system, and the DD-21 destroyer, have highlighted the tough budget decisions ahead. As the Congressional Budget Office (CBO) has noted, current and projected Procurement spending is approximately $30 billion per year below the CBO's estimate for sustaining current planned purchases (U.S. Congressional Budget Office, 2000, pp. 13–24). This "bow wave" effect is illustrated by Table 1.3 and Figure 1.1.

These discussions of the strategy-resource mismatch have largely been framed in terms of resources rather than in terms of strategy.[13] This emphasis on funding levels, however, has downplayed the importance of strategy. A strategy that better links what we *say* is impor-

---

[8]For assessments of the impact of military operations during the 1990s, see U.S. General Accounting Office (2000), U.S.

General Accounting Office (1999), and U.S. Congressional Budget Office (1999).

[9]In particular, see Gouré and Ranney (1999). See also U.S. Congressional Budget Office (1997).

[10]For an excellent example of this critique with regard to ground forces, see Macgregor (1997), p. 4. Macgregor argues for brigade-sized joint task forces that are smaller, more mobile, and more adaptable than the current division structure. He contends, "To date, warfighting organizations for the Army of the future look much like the force structures in the past and present."

[11]As argued in Davis (1994), pp. 39–50, current major formations are ill suited for future needs and those building blocks of capability need to be reengineered.

[12]For example, see Gouré and Ranney (1999), Macgregor (1997), and Owens (2000).

[13]Flournoy (2000) is a notable exception to this trend.

Table 1.3

Average Annual Procurement Spending by Platform
(in numbers of purchases)

| | Average Annual Purchases | |
Platform	1975–1990	1991–2000
Tanks, artillery, and other armored vehicles	2,083	145
Scout and attack helicopters	78	7
Utility helicopters	109	69
Battle force ships	19	7
Fighter/attack aircraft, Navy	111	42
Fighter/attack aircraft, Air Force	238	28
Tactical and strategic airlift	31	15
Tankers	5	1
Heavy bombers	7	1

SOURCE: U.S. Congressional Budget Office (2000).

tant to what actually *is* important (that is, what we buy) will help mitigate these kind of dramatic budgetary dilemmas.

DIFFICULTIES IN MAPPING STRATEGY TO BUDGET

As the preceding discussion illustrates, there are significant difficulties in attempting to link strategy to resources. The four major budgetary categories (Personnel; Operation and Maintenance [O&M]; Procurement; and Research, Test, Development, and Evaluation [RTD&E])[14] do not map readily to the three strategy categories. More specific examinations of budget titles or major programs do yield some insights, but making broader connections between budgets and strategy, however, proved elusive.

The three prongs of the Shape, Respond, and Prepare Now military strategy each contain principal sub-objectives, or key tenants. These tenets are illustrated in Table 1.4.

---

[14]See the DoD Comptroller Web site, http://www.dtic.mil/comptroller, for detailed information about the structure and specifics of the DoD budget, including current and recent fiscal years' budget submissions.

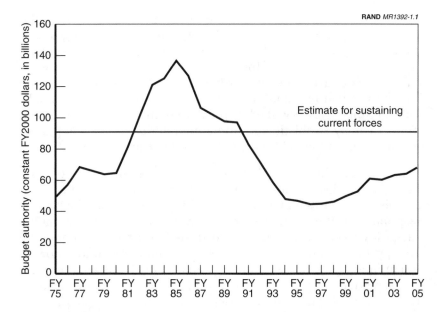

SOURCES: U.S. Congressional Budget Office (2000) and U.S. Department of Defense (1999).

Figure 1.1—Historical and Projected Levels of Procurement Spending

Table 1.4

Key Tenets of the U.S. Defense Strategy

Shaping the International Environment	Responding to the Full Spectrum of Crises	Preparing Now for an Uncertain Future
Promoting regional stability	Deterring aggression or coercion in crisis (immediate deterrence)	Conducting focused modernization
Preventing or reducing conflicts and other threats	Conducting small-scale contingencies	Pursuing RMA/ transformation
Deterring aggression or coercion (general deterrence)	Fighting and winning MTWs	Exploiting the revolution in business affairs
		Hedging against unlikely but significant future threats

Many military activities naturally cluster around these key tenets. For example, combined exercises, military-to-military exchanges, and grants to help transform the militaries of *transition states*—chiefly China and Russia, but also India and others—can promote regional stability. Similarly, the air strikes and other activities during Operation Allied Force fall into the category of conducting small-scale contingencies (SSCs) while the development and procurement of increasingly sophisticated unmanned aerial vehicles is part of pursuing Revolution in Military Affairs (RMA)/transformation.

Unfortunately, however, these sorts of connections do not hold throughout a close examination of the budget. Many activities, such as training, maintenance, and recruiting, cut across the Shape, Respond, and Prepare Now strategy. Moreover, the major budget categories that appear to directly correlate to the three prongs of the strategy in fact do not: O&M does not equal "respond," nor do Procurement plus RDT&E equal "prepare now." Put another way, precisely what constitutes "shape," for instance, is a matter of judgment. Is, for instance, the U.S. deployment in Kosovo shaping the international security environment or responding to a current crisis? It was initially a response to crisis, but the Kosovo Force today is certainly more of a shaping operation. How do you differentiate between those two stages? The fact that there are, literally, thousands of program elements within the defense budget makes the very effort to connect the strategy to expenditures a daunting one.[15]

Ultimately, it is extremely difficult, if not impossible, to definitely map defense expenditures to the current strategy. More to the point, because so many expenditures and activities cut across the Shape, Respond, and Prepare Now prongs of the U.S. strategy, almost anything can be justified in those categories. If almost anything can be included, virtually nothing is excluded, and as a result, the strategy is of relatively little help in either posing or helping to make major decisions about weapons, operations, or missions. In addition, this exercise illustrates the fact that the mechanism between the strategy and the underlying PPBS is weak. Activities between high

---

[15]For one explicit attempt to establish a programmatic link between the 1997 strategy and resource allocations decisions, see Hillestad and Davis (1998).

strategy and program analysis have been poor and difficult decisions involving weapons systems have been rare.

BUILDING A FRAMEWORK TO DEVELOP STRATEGY FOR U.S. FORCES

The difficulty of mapping strategy to budget shows the need for a framework that better links them together. Such a framework will attempt to develop a mechanism that allows strategic choices to be more closely reflected in resource decisionmaking. This framework approach is different from other recent efforts to rethink the defense strategy. Most of the previous exercises have centered on developing strategy based on some hierarchy of interests,[16] or developing alternative model strategies and evaluating their effectiveness (Flournoy, 2000). These efforts are important, but they are closely related to current debates. In contrast, this study attempts to establish a framework that is useful in developing strategies across different time periods, preferences, and circumstances. This approach allows the framework—and therefore any resulting strategy—to adapt to changing circumstances.

The starting-point for the analysis is the recognition that any U.S. military strategy must answer a number of questions:

- What is the rationale and objective of U.S. defense policy?
- What kinds of operations will U.S. forces conduct?
- What kind of operational challenges will U.S. forces face?
- How will the future security environment impact the strategy?
- What capabilities will allies bring to bear?
- What new or enhanced U.S. capabilities will be required?
- What will be the appropriate active/reserve mix?
- What capabilities can U.S. forces de-emphasize?

---

[16]See, for example, Rice (2000), pp. 45–62, and Carter (1999–2000), pp. 101–123.

The answers to the previous questions will begin to highlight the important choices policymakers face in attempting to develop a strategy for U.S. military forces.

Strategy development has objective and subjective aspects, and a key goal of this report is to craft an adaptable framework that accounts for both. This framework is hardly a "strategy machine," for such a creation would be impossible. What the framework seeks to do is to lay out the elements of strategy in a logical and transparent way. It seeks to integrate perspectives that are both top-down (for example, the world view of key decisionmakers) and bottom-up (for example, sets of capabilities for conducting activities such as environment shaping or missile defense). In short, the framework provides a space in which decisionmakers can first display strategic options and their inherent tradeoffs, then debate the merits of these competing choices, and then finally decide on a specific strategy. The framework is displayed in Figure 1.2.

A number of steps are involved in crafting the framework. The first step is elucidating preferences about strategic emphases. Suppose a decisionmaker wanted to give strategic priority to policing global instability, or to preparing for competition with China, or another specific challenge? We call these preferences *themes* and in this report we consider six that span a broad spectrum of strategic objectives, rationales, and potential contingencies:

- Ambitious Shaping
- Countering Rogues
- Protecting the Homeland
- Countering New Dangers
- Preparing for China
- Policing Instability.

The framework then links those themes to the respective force postures (that is, how to structure, deploy, and position U.S. forces, and how to use those forces for fighting) and special capability packages (for example, missile defense, information operations, or stability operations) that are necessary to carry out those themes. No single theme alone amounts to a strategy, but rather several themes could

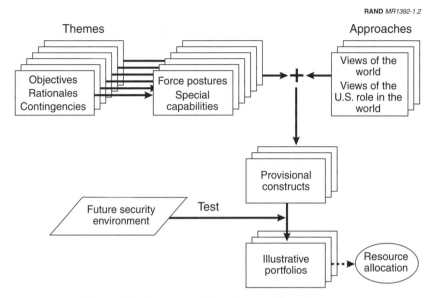

RAND *MR1392-1.2*

Figure 1.2—Framework for Strategy Development

be combined in different ways to provide the rudimentary foundation of a strategy.

In the next step, we look illustratively at three pairs of themes, labeled "Provisional Constructs" in Figure 1.2, which reflect different views of the world and of the U.S. role within it (shown as "Approaches" in the figure). The framework then provides ways to test these *constructs* against the drivers of the future security environment, examining both the relevance and feasibility of each construct. Based on those tests, the constructs can then be refined. Looking across several of the refined constructs provides an indication of which capabilities are relatively common and which are less necessary, and, especially, what key choices are implied by moving toward one construct or another. The refined constructs can be portrayed as *illustrative portfolios* that suggest where to invest resources, where to divest resources, and where to maintain existing capabilities. Herein lies the crucial link between strategy and resources.

It should be stressed again that the framework is not deterministic. The themes and constructs used in this report are illustrations designed to cover a rich range of possibilities and to catch some of the flavor that seems implicit in the current debate about the future of U.S. defense. The illustrations are intended to make the framework more vivid; they are not to be regarded as recommendations, nor is the utility of the framework limited to current debates or circumstances.

Chapter Two

ARTICULATING STRATEGIC THEMES

The basic building blocks of the strategy-development framework are the strategic themes. These themes emphasize particular aspects of U.S. defense policy, such as countering rogue states or protecting the homeland. As such, they are emphases, and not strategies; any strategy would combine aspects of several themes that are mixed in various ways. The themes that are articulated cannot be entirely independent of each other but nevertheless should be distinct enough to have different implications for the defense program. And, for purposes of illustration, we wanted the set of themes to span a wide range of possible national security objectives and future military operations.

The six themes—Ambitious Shaping, Countering Rogues, Protecting the Homeland, Countering New Dangers, Preparing for China, and Policing Instability—cover a wide range of choices conerning the United States' role in the world and its defense underpinnings.

AMBITIOUS SHAPING

This theme is based on the rationale that a formative moment in the world's political geography is happening now. The world's *core* of nation-states—those states that are democracies and have market economies—is strong and growing larger, and much of the globe's political future will turn on whether major transition states—chiefly China and Russia, but also India and others—remain on the path toward democracy and economic openness. Thus, the task associated with this theme is twofold: to turn U.S. allies into full partners in shaping the world before us, and, especially, to devote special attention to large transition states (in particular, China and Russia) to do what we can to ensure that their transitions succeed.[1] The instruments for this environment-shaping may be political and economic ones to an even greater degree than they are military ones. Operationally, this theme emphasizes expeditionary operations to decisively defeat potential adversaries and engagement activities of all sorts targeted on both allies and transition states.

This theme seeks to use the U.S. military to build connections with the transition states through combined exercises, coalition operations, and military-to-military contacts and exchanges.[2] At the same time, America's ability to shape the future security environment also depends on continued and unquestioned U.S. military strength.

COUNTERING ROGUES

This theme is rooted in the premise that rogue states (for example, Iraq, Iran, and North Korea) will continue to be a threat to the United States.[3] Rogue states are more or less alienated from the global system and are considered to be dangerous, but their military capabilities are somewhat limited. Because they are militarily weaker than the United States, rogues may resort to asymmetric measures, such as reliance on weapons of mass destruction (WMD) as a threat and, possibly, as a fact of war. More generally, rogue states will seek to exploit the United States' Achilles' heels (for example, through anti-access strategies accompanied by short-warning attacks and quick movement into cities).

The objective of this theme is thus to deter and, if required, defeat those rogues. Operationally, it does not necessarily assume that

---

[1]So-called realist theorists are skeptical of the prospects for tight cooperation among major states because all of them live in a "security dilemma": They are trapped in a ceaseless struggle to assure their security by increasing their power relative to other states. The classic statement is Herz (1951), fn. 24. States will form alliances to "balance" possible aggressors, but they will necessarily also be sensitive to the power of their alliance partners. See Walt (1987).

[2]For an extended discussion of possible instruments for shaping, see *1998 Strategic Assessment: Engaging Power for Peace* (1998), Chapter 2.

[3]A backlash to current U.S. dominance, however benign the exercise of it may be, might come from both states and non-state actors. See, for instance, Huntington (1999), p. 35, or Layne (1998), pp. 8–28.

countering rogues will require future Desert Storms. It does imply, however, a greater attention to countering the threat of WMD attacks and to building combat capabilities that include strong projection forces, forward stationing, and the ability to defeat anti-access strategies.

PROTECTING THE HOMELAND

This theme focuses on the need for the United States to worry less about the world, which seems to be coming along reasonably well, and be concerned more about itself. The objective of this theme, then, is to elevate the importance of protecting the U.S. territory and its citizens. By embracing this theme, one may or may not believe that the United States should pull back somewhat from its obligations and deployments abroad. The theme is not, in itself, isolationist, but rather an expression of the belief that homeland defense has been shortchanged.

Operationally, this theme focuses on defending against missiles, countering WMD and major non-WMD terrorism, and protecting the information systems of the United States and its allies, and also on dealing with the civilian consequences of these threats and, conceivably, actual attacks. This would entail a greater role for the military (especially the Reserves and National Guard) in homeland defense of but also necessitates the ability to conduct expeditionary operations to eliminate threats overseas. This theme would also require a great deal of coordination between the DoD and nonmilitary agencies.

COUNTERING NEW DANGERS

This theme centers on confronting the new and largely unconventional challenges in the global system. Its rationale is that the positive aspects of globalization (for example, free-market capitalism, democratization, and increasing zones of peace and prosperity)[4] will continue as will U.S. military superiority. States that might be potential adversaries of the United States are deterred. The United States

---

[4]See Chapter Five for a discussion of the positive and negative aspects of globalization.

thus has both the need and the luxury to focus on unfamiliar threats, most of them *transnational*—that is, threats resulting not from the actions of nation-states but rather from the underside of globalization. The objective of this theme is to prevent and, if need be, deter such new threats.

Operationally, this theme would focus on countering WMD terrorism and non-WMD terrorism by non-state actors, the trafficking of illegal drugs, and information warfare. As with the Protecting the Homeland theme, these sorts of activities would require a great deal of coordination between the DoD and nonmilitary agencies.

PREPARING FOR CHINA

This theme centers on preparing for the emergence of an economic and military near peer. The rationale is that, in the long run, of all the transition states only China can pose anything like a peer threat to the United States.[5] This does not presume that China will be an enemy, only that China's emerging capabilities will determine the benchmark by which U.S. forces should be judged, and that China's own military growth will be less threatening if it takes place in the recognized shadow of U.S. superiority. This theme's objective is to prevent Chinese ascendancy by making U.S. superiority clear, and to shape China into a true strategic partner.

Operationally, this theme would emphasize the continued capacity to project military power into Asia, interoperability with regional allies, and defense against China's medium- and long-range missiles. It would mean staunch support for friendly regional states such as Japan, Korea, and Taiwan. And it would mean increasing, rather than decreasing, basing options for operations in the Asia-Pacific region. The focus of power projection would likely be on naval and aerospace operations.

---

[5]Realist theorists would say that states must care about their relative position in the world, and the most important aspects of that position are their status and prestige relative to other states. States will "keep up with the Joneses," and, moreover, as their power increases, so will their aspirations. In Kapstein and Mastanduno (1999), see Schweller, Chapter 2, in particular.

POLICING INSTABILITY

Like the Countering New Dangers theme, this theme addresses the underside of otherwise favorable trends. Motivated by the expectation that the positive aspects of globalization will continue and that U.S. strength will continue to deter major state-centered threats, this theme also hypothesizes that terrorism (with and without WMD), while a factor, is muted by global economic growth and by U.S. military power.

This theme aims to lead coalitions of willing allies to preserve and restore order in those places where the "good" aspects of globalization fail to take root. It would concentrate on multilateral stability operations and engagement activities of all sorts. This theme reflects much of the recent past when, lacking serious enemies, the United States has had both the capacity and the discretion to decide where and when it would intervene to police instability.

Chapter Three

LINKING THEMES TO FORCE POSTURES AND CAPABILITIES

Because the themes discussed in Chapter Two are fairly distinct from one another, they tend to require different military capabilities. For example, the Policing Instability theme would require less conventional combat capability than, say, the Countering Rogues theme. Similarly, the Protecting the Homeland theme would probably require greater emphasis on missile defense than would the Ambitious Shaping theme.

If the themes truly cover a wide range of strategic choices, then scanning across them should identify those capabilities that are relevant across many themes and those capabilities that have a narrower focus and are important only for a particular theme or two. But how should "capabilities" be defined? The term encompasses weaponry, types of forces, and types of operations. But attempting to separate the capabilities according to those three categories quickly produced a blizzard of complexity. Moreover, some of the capabilities identified in this way were major components of forces, while others were much more specialized; it was like comparing apples and oranges and we ran the risk of obscuring, rather than highlighting, the critical choices.

In the end, we defined three *force postures* and seven *special capability packages.* As was done elsewhere in creating the strategy framework, this definition of postures and capabilities was a compromise between capturing reality and not overcomplicating the analysis. The three force postures reflect basic choices on how to structure, deploy, and position U.S. forces and use those forces in fighting. The special capability packages combine weapons, forces, platforms, and missions, but they are also sets of resources that are necessary to accomplish particular types of operations and missions.

DEFINING THE FORCE POSTURES

The following three force postures are the basic building blocks of defense.

Traditionally Configured Combat Forces

This force posture generally reflects the current disposition of U.S. military forces: division building blocks for ground forces, traditional aircraft and air forces, and carrier-centered naval operations. This posture would also entail a traditional forward presence of overseas bases and stationary prepositioned equipment. Reserves would serve primarily as backup combat power. Conventional combat forces will have inherent capabilities, such as fighting and winning MTWs.

Expeditionary Forces

This force posture envisions more-modular and rapidly deployable forces capable of responding to diverse contingencies around the world: brigade building blocks for ground forces, multirole aircraft in a fully implemented Aerospace Expeditionary Force (AEF), and fewer carrier-centered naval operations. Traditionally configured combat forces would be re-engineered for more expeditionary missions. This transformation has been referred to as part of an "Era A RMA": exploiting within-reach technology to solve problems that are visible now (Davis et al., 1998). This force transformation focuses on the next ten years or so.

This posture would also entail a flexible forward presence consisting of fewer permanently stationed units abroad and more prepositioned equipment afloat. Reserves would augment active component deployment capabilities as well as maintain conventional combat capabilities. Expeditionary forces will have inherent capabilities, such as rapid power projection, conducting forced-entry operations, and countering anti-access.

Forces-After-Next Focus

This posture envisions a more radical shift in the nature of military forces and would emphasize leap-ahead technology. This transformation, sometimes referred to as "Era B RMA," is focused beyond 2010 and preparing for it is a matter of *hedging:* developing a diverse set of capabilities that will allow U.S. forces to adapt in the years ahead (Davis et al., 1998).[1] The outcome of this process is unclear and alternative concepts may prove out, but some proponents have in mind ground and air forces built out of smaller-than-brigade/wing-building blocks and naval operations using smaller platforms such as Streetfighter. The expectation is that there will be a premium placed on dispersal and long reach. These force postures are summarized in Table 3.1.

These force postures are intended to be serious alternatives, and it is important that they retain their distinctiveness. A Traditionally Configured Forces posture is different from an Expeditionary Forces posture, and so, too, would an Expeditionary Forces posture probably differ from a Forces-After-Next Focus posture. It would be all too easy conceptually, and all too tempting organizationally, to blur the distinctions. And, of course, the path to the goal of one posture might pass through another. If U.S. forces are now for the most part traditionally configured, with some expeditionary elements, a chosen path to the forces-after-next posture might for a time look like an expeditionary posture in many respects.

DEFINING THE SPECIAL CAPABILITY PACKAGES

Like force postures, the special capability packages combine weapons, forces, platforms, and missions, but they also combine sets of resources that are necessary to accomplish particular types of operations and missions. For example, the capabilities necessary to conduct missile defense, environment shaping, and countering

---

[1]U.S. Joint Forces Command (USJFCOM) is the chief advocate for jointness and its approach to the RMA is similar to the Era A and Era B model. USJFCOM documents speak of *evolutionary concepts* to shape the force of the next decade and *revolutionary concepts* to shape what the USJFCOM terms "America's Joint Force After Next."

Table 3.1

Characteristics and Capabilities of Alternative Force Postures

Force Postures	Key Characteristics	Inherent Capabilities
Traditionally Configured Combat Forces	Divisional buildings blocks for ground forces, traditional aircraft and air forces, carrier battle group (CVBG)–centered naval operations, traditional forward presence, stationary preposition, reserves as backup combat power	Fight and win MTWs Conduct SSCs
Expeditionary Forces	More-modular brigade building blocks for ground forces, multirole aircraft, fully implemented AEF, fewer CVBG-centered naval operations, flexible forward presence, prepositioned afloat, reserves increase rotation base	Rapid power projection Conduct forced-entry operations Counter anti-access
Forces-After-Next Focus	Radical force transformation embracing Era B RMA; outcome unclear but could include ground and air forces built out of smaller-than-brigade/wing building blocks and naval operations using smaller platforms such as Streetfighter; premium on dispersal and long reach	Rapid power projection with small logistical footprint Operate in network-centric environment Secure homeland

transnational threats such as crime, illegal drugs, and terrorism are somewhat unique packages.

If the force postures represent basic choices, then the special capability packages might be thought of as more specialized capability add-ons. The capability packages are relatively commensurate with one another. Most would require spending money on some things at the expense of others, but in some cases the "cost" may lie more in required organizational changes in operations and personnel tempo or in the opportunity (and, perhaps, readiness) costs of using forces in one way as opposed to another.

The special capability packages are not subsets of the three force postures, but instead highlight some of the key sets of capabilities that could shape U.S. military forces in a significant way during the coming years. If, for example, Missile Defense and Countering WMD are very important for a particular theme, whereas Stability Operations and Nontraditional Missions are less important, the strategic choices suggested by the theme could have major repercussions on the posture and possibly the structure of U.S. forces. An emphasis on countering transnational threats and information operations, on the other hand, would lead to a very different force posture.

We designated seven special capability packages. These packages are not intended to be comprehensive, but to highlight the key choices and tradeoffs inherent in the different themes. The packages are summarized in Table 3.2.

Table 3.2
Key Characteristics of Special Capability Packages

Package	Characteristics
Stability Operations	Peace and paramilitary tasks, soldier-centered RMA
Missile Defense	NMD, TMD, strategic deterrence
Countering WMD	CIP, force protection (home and abroad), consequence management, civil support
Countering Transnational Threats (crime, drugs, terrorism)	Aerial surveillance, naval and air interdiction, HUMINT, combined operations
Information Operations	Space protection, IA, PSYOPS, perception management
Environment Shaping	Combined exercises, planning, military contacts, and other activities to increase interoperability and to strengthen alliances and coalitions; security assistance (FID and such) and other activities to increase capacity of partners
Nontraditional Missions	Humanitarian relief (airlift, aid, hospital ships, and such), activities related to civil affairs, and other activities to deal with disease and natural disasters

Conducting Stability Operations

These capabilities are required to conduct peace enforcement and peacekeeping operations. They include tasks such as disestablishing a guerrilla roadblock and conducting mounted and dismounted security patrols. A soldier-centered RMA focused on developing weapons and equipment for urban combat and other aspects of stability operations will also be key.

Conducting Missile Defense

The research and development (R&D) for, experimentation with, and, eventually, deployment of missile defense systems will call on a broad range of capabilities. There are two general categories of potential systems: national missile defense (NMD) and theater missile defense (TMD). Significant barriers remain to the deployment of effective NMD and TMD systems; the strategic and budgetary priority assigned to these systems, however, should have a corresponding (positive or negative) impact on their development. Some level of strategic deterrence will also remain a necessary component of any deployed missile defense system.

Countering WMD

These capabilities focus on deterring, preventing, and dealing with the aftermath of the use of weapons of mass destruction. They include proactive measures such as cooperative threat-reduction programs with Russia. Key measures to defend against a WMD attack include critical infrastructure protection (CIP), counterintelligence, and force protection (home and abroad). Civil support and consequence management are critical in responding to a successful WMD attack.

Countering Transnational Threats

Mitigating the effects of crime, illegal drugs, terrorism, and other transnational threats will require common sets of military capabilities. They include technical capabilities, such as aerial surveillance and satellite imagery, and more-traditional military activities, such as naval and air interdiction and combined operations, but also increased human intelligence (HUMINT).

Conducting Information Operations

Protecting U.S. and allied information systems will be a major emphasis in the years ahead. As a result, information assurance (IA) and the protection of satellites and other systems in outer space will play a major role in defending against attacks on U.S. information systems. However, offensive activities, such as psychological operations (PSYOPS) and perception management (activities designed to influence the beliefs and actions of foreign government officials and/or foreign people), also will be important.

Conducting Environment Shaping

Engagement activities require a diverse set of capabilities. From formal alliance forces and alliance planning to combined exercises with traditional or nontraditional coalition partners, as well as military-to-military contacts and exchanges, environment shaping works to increase interoperability and coordination. Security-assistance activities, such as support for foreign internal defense (FID), work to increase partner capacity.

Conducting Nontraditional Missions

Humanitarian relief operations, such as food airlifts, security to assure the equitable distribution of food, and the use of hospital ships for medical care, provide avenues for the military to operate in nontraditional ways. These sorts of operations combined with other activities, such as those related to civil affairs, allow the military to assist in dealing with the aftereffects of natural disasters or large-scale outbreaks of famine or disease.

ASSESSING THE RELATIVE IMPORTANCE OF FORCE POSTURES AND CAPABILITIES

With the postures and capability packages defined, the next step is to identify, for each theme, whether a given package is "very important," "important," or "less important" for carrying out the theme.

A "very important" force posture or special capability package is one that needs greater emphasis strategically than other postures or capabilities and probably needs greater emphasis in terms of resources for a specific theme. For example, missile defense is very important to the Protecting the Homeland theme because the focus of that theme is on protecting the U.S. territory and its citizens from attack.

An "important" force posture or capability package needs continued emphasis for a specific theme. For instance, although the Countering Rogues theme is centered on defeating hostile nations with military force, the Environment Shaping capability will remain an important component of that theme because it helps to forestall the emergence of new rogues. Environment Shaping will therefore need continued strategic and budgetary emphasis.

There are also some capabilities and force postures that are "less important" and could be de-emphasized for various themes. For the Policing Instability theme, for example, missile defense is less important than other capability packages and would therefore receive lower strategic priority and lower priority in terms of resource decisions.

Assessing the relative importance of the three force postures and seven capability packages to the themes led to some interesting conclusions about each theme. Table 3.3 summarizes the ranking of the force postures and capability packages against the themes.

Assessing Postures and Capabilities for the Ambitious Shaping Theme

The most useful force posture for the Ambitious Shaping theme is one that is oriented toward expeditionary operations. Traditionally Configured Combat Forces also becomes important as the U.S. military moves toward an expeditionary posture. A Forces-After-Next

Table 3.3

Ranking of Force Postures and Capabilities for Each Theme

	Theme					
	Ambitious Shaping	Countering Rogues	Protecting the Homeland	Countering New Dangers	Preparing for China	Policing Instability
Force Posture						
Traditionally Configured Combat Forces	Important	Important	Less Important	Less Important	Less Important	Important
Expeditionary Forces	Very Important	Very Important	Important	Very Important	Important	Very Important
Forces-After-Next Focus	Less Important	Less Important	Very Important	Important	Very Important	Less Important
Special Capability Package						
Stability Operations	Important	Important	Less Important	Less Important	Less Important	Very Important
Missile Defense	Less Important	Very Important	Very Important	Less Important	Very Important	Less Important
Countering WMD	Important	Very Important	Very Important	Very Important	Important	Less Important
Countering Transnational Threats	Important	Important	Very Important	Very Important	Less Important	Important
Information Operations	Very Important	Very Important	Very Important	Very Important	Very Important	Important
Environment Shaping	Very Important	Important	Less Important	Important	Very Important	Very Important
Nontraditional Missions	Important	Less Important	Less Important	Less Important	Less Important	Very Important

Focus posture is less important, however, because there is not a tremendous need to radically transform the already-preeminent U.S. military.

In terms of special capability packages, Information Operations and Environment Shaping need the most emphasis because of their critical roles in strengthening alliances and coalitions as well as in helping to bring transition states to more-favorable positions. Stability Operations, Countering WMD, Countering Transnational Threats, and Nontraditional Missions are also important because they work to support the objectives of this theme, and therefore need continued strategic and resource emphasis. Missile Defense is the only special capability package that is less important for the Ambitious Shaping theme. Although R&D on NMD systems, and especially on TMD systems, continues to have some importance, it is lower on the priority scale than are the other sets of capabilities. Experimentation or deployment of these systems, similarly, has a much lower strategic or budgetary priority.

Assessing Postures and Capabilities for the Countering Rogues Theme

Because of this theme's emphasis on defeating Achilles' heel and anti-access strategies, Expeditionary Forces is the most appropriate posture. Traditionally Configured Combat Forces is also a useful posture while expeditionary units are being developed. The Forces-After-Next Focus posture, on the other hand, is not as important because the weight of the theme is on defeating challenges that are more in the near term.

Missile Defense, Countering WMD, and Information Operations are the special capability packages that need the most emphasis. They work directly to meet the objectives of the theme. Stability Operations, Countering Transnational Threats, and Environment Shaping need continued emphasis so that the U.S. military has the capability to deal with the aftermath of change in a rogue-state regime, defend against state-sponsored terrorism, and conduct engagement activities to help turn rogues (or potential rogues) into transition states.

Assessing Postures and Capabilities for the Protecting the Homeland Theme

Given the emphasis on protecting the U.S. territory and its citizens, the most appropriate posture for this theme is the Forces-After-Next Focus. This would put U.S. forces in a better position to counter WMD, transnational threats, or attacks to the information systems of the United States or its allies. An Expeditionary Forces posture would be useful in the transition to a Forces-After-Next Focus posture, whereas a Traditionally Configured Combat Forces posture is not that helpful.

Missile Defense, Countering WMD, Countering Transnational Threats, and Information Operations are the most important special capability packages for protecting the homeland. Stability Operations, Environment Shaping, and Nontraditional Missions are less important and can be de-emphasized strategically and in terms of resources.

Assessing Postures and Capabilities for the Countering New Dangers Theme

An Expeditionary Forces posture is the most appropriate for this theme because U.S. forces need to be able to rapidly deploy and defeat non-state actors conducting terrorist acts, illegal drug trafficking, and other activities that cut across state boundaries. A Forces-After-Next Focus posture is also important to develop a diverse set of military capabilities that will allow U.S. forces to deal with increasingly diffuse transnational threats in the years ahead. A Traditionally Configured Combat Forces posture is much less useful.

For the particular challenges inherent in this theme, Countering WMD, Countering Transnational Threats, and Information Operations are the capability packages that are the most relevant and therefore need the greatest emphasis. Environment Shaping needs continued emphasis because maintaining and deepening alliance and coalition relationships will be important in these types of operations. Stability Operations, Missile Defense, and Nontraditional Missions are less important because they do not play a major role in dealing with the threats associated with this theme.

Assessing Postures and Capabilities for the Preparing for China Theme

With the focus on the emergence of a near peer in China, not imme-diately but in the post-2010 time frame, the most appropriate posture is the Forces-After-Next Focus. Passing through an Era A expeditionary force posture on the way to an Era B transformation posture is also important. A Traditionally Configured Forces posture is much less important as the military adapts to this new strategic emphasis.

Missile Defense, Information Operations, and Environment Shaping are very important capability packages because they, respectively, protect the United States and its allies against missile threats, work to favorably influence Chinese perceptions of U.S. actions in Asia, and attempt to make China a partner while building up coalition partners in the region in the event the effort to make China a partner is unsuc-cessful. Countering WMD is important especially if the U.S.-China relationship becomes hostile. Stability Operations, Transnational Threats, and Nontraditional Missions are less important because of the nature of military activities in this theme.

Assessing Postures and Capabilities for the Policing Instability Theme

An Expeditionary Forces posture is the most important for this theme because of its emphasis on the ability to conduct numerous SSCs. A Traditionally Configured Combat Forces posture is still useful because those forces can quickly adapt to the mostly lower-end challenges of policing instability. A Forces-After-Next Focus posture is less important because the military does not need to radically transform in order to meet the coming challenges.

Stability Operations, Environment Shaping, and Nontraditional Missions are the most relevant special capability packages for this theme. Countering Transnational Threats and Information Opera-tions are also important because they, respectively, help to defend against possible threats to stability and influence adversarial and indigenous opinions about U.S. goals and objectives. Missile Defense and Countering WMD are less important capabilities because there is little danger of high-end military threats.

INTERMEDIATE OBSERVATIONS

At this point, it is worth identifying those force postures and special capability packages that are broadly required across themes and those that have more-limited application. The Traditionally Configured Combat Forces and the Forces-After-Next Focus postures rank "less important" for three themes, and the Traditionally Configured Combat Forces posture is "very important" for no theme. A Forces-After-Next Focus posture is very important for two themes—Protecting the Homeland and Preparing for China. Not surprisingly, perhaps, the Expeditionary Forces posture is ranked "very important" for four themes and ranked "important" for two themes.

Four special capability packages—Countering WMD, Countering Transnational Threats, Information Operations, and Environment Shaping—rank "very important" or "important" for at least four themes. Two other capabilities packages—Stability Operations and Missile Defense—rank "very important" or "important" for at least three themes. Only Nontraditional Missions rank "less important" for four or more themes.

The framework thus begins to identify a core set of capabilities that seem necessary across a wide range of emphases in U.S. defense strategy. By also identifying those capabilities that are required for only one or two themes, the framework begins to suggest which choices about capabilities depend greatly on the particularities of strategy and which do not. It begins to do what current strategy does not: enable strategic choices to drive programmatic ones.

Given how we have illustrated the choices in this scenario, the most-difficult choice would appear to be regarding missile defense because the Missile Defense special capability package is very important for three of the themes but is less important for the other three. The rankings underscore the point that deciding whether or not to move ahead with certain capabilities has very significant implications for defense strategy.

Chapter Four

FORMING STRATEGIC CONSTRUCTS

American strategy plainly turns on how U.S. leaders view the world and the role of the United States within it. This philosophical approach to defense policy significantly influences those leaders' strategic choices. Strategic themes typically reflect an emphasis on particular issues, but a policymaker's vantage point needs to be broader than that.

With that in mind, we next describe three generic strategic constructs that reflect different perspectives of the role that the United States plays in the world. We then rate the importance of the force postures and special capability packages, discussed in Chapter Three, relative to each of the three generic constructs in order to create what we call "provisional constructs." Those provisional constructs will be further refined, as discussed in Chapter Six, by taking into account assumptions about the future security environment.

DEVELOPING THE CONSTRUCTS

While the themes discussed in this report remain the basic building blocks of a strategic framework, the next step is to use them to build something that resembles a strategy. The result is a "strategic construct." Such constructs are developed by mixing a bottom-up view of the themes with a top-down perspective of the various approaches to defining the role of the United States in the world. Combining the six themes into pairs produces three constructs that illustrate distinct ways in which the United States can formulate its defense strategy. The three constructs are Focus on Key Responsibilities, U.S. Multilateral Leadership, and Protecting an Essential Core.

Components of the Focus on Key Responsibilities Construct

This construct combines the attributes of the Countering Rogues and Preparing for China themes. It posits that the United States has a distinct position with special historical responsibilities in the new era. The United States must confront the most demanding current and future security challenges—with friends, if possible, but alone, if necessary. These challenges include dealing with hostile states that have WMD and the means to deliver them; addressing threats to world energy supplies; maintaining peace in regions that are both vital and potentially insecure (for instance, key areas in East and Southwest Asia); and addressing the emergence of a powerful China. The United States must focus its defense policy and resources accordingly.

U.S. forces must be capable of conducting increasingly difficult and violent high-intensity operations against adversaries who have access to spreading technology. Those forces must adapt their doctrines and structures to exploit information technology rapidly and completely, even if doing so makes coalition operations more difficult. The United States must spare no effort to neutralize at least the low-end WMD/ballistic missile threat.

The ability to respond to major crises in East and Southwest Asia is a crucial test for those forces and their peacetime deployment. The United States will take advantage of the growing willingness of European allies, via the European Union, to conduct peacekeeping and other lower-intensity operations in and immediately around Europe by reducing (but not ending) its own involvement in these sorts of operations. The United States is willing to see its relationship with NATO evolve to create a division of labor, with the Europeans handling lower-end operations in Europe and its environs and the United States handling the bulk of higher-end operations outside Europe.

The United States is prepared to organize and lead coalitions when it is compelled to act, but not at the expense of being able to modernize its forces to meet high-intensity needs. Era A and Era B transformations (which are discussed in Chapter Three) are both important, but the principal focus will be to exploit Era A activities that center on re-engineering the military to reduce personnel and related costs while maintaining, and even extending, functional capabilities (Davis et al., 1998).

This construct will attempt to reduce operations tempo and its dele-terious effects by being more selective about the frequency and char-acter of its participation in SSCs. The United States cannot count on its allies to handle threats that exploit America's Achilles' heels or handle threats from peer competitors, but those allies should be willing and able to handle lesser contingencies. Finally, the American public supports the substantial, and even increased, defense spend-ing required by this construct.

Components of the U.S. Multilateral Leadership Construct

This construct is composed of the Ambitious Shaping and Policing Instability themes. From this perspective, the recent past holds sev-eral important lessons for U.S. defense strategy: The future of major transition states (that is, China and Russia) is far from clear; instabil-ity remains high from the Balkans through Africa and from the Middle East to South, Southeast, and Northeast Asia; the American public expects allies to bear more burdens and risks, and may op-pose the use of force if U.S. allies do not bear more of the defense burden; and high-intensity conflict is unlikely (because of U.S. supe-riority and deterrence), whereas SSC demands will persist.

SSCs normally demand multilateral approaches. Multilateralism, in turn, both contributes to and benefits from active, forward engage-ment, not only with allies but also with transition states. Thus, re-sponding to the instability of the current environment through the use of multilateral SSCs dovetails with the aim of encouraging more-responsible allied and transition powers.

Interoperability and Era A transformation activities are essential to increase military capabilities; thus, the capabilities gap between the United States and its allies can and must be reduced. Era B RMA is less crucial because of the near-term vision of this construct. The United States responds to the WMD threat through reducing insta-bility and strengthening multilateral cooperation with allies and transition states.

This construct is not intended as a substitute for having strong military forces for deterrence, but rather expresses an emphasis on the United States working with partners rather than unilaterally taking on worldwide responsibilities.

Components of the Protecting an Essential Core Construct

The themes of Protecting the Homeland and Countering New Dangers form this construct. Broadly speaking, international trends are favorable, and U.S. military superiority is sufficient to protect traditional interests (for example, U.S. territory) from traditional threats (for example, foreign military forces). Transition states are on the right track, instability is abating in key regions, and allies are taking on more responsibility. Military instruments and operations are not the only way or even the preferred way of coping with most challenges. MTWs are highly unlikely, but deterring them is possible without expending great effort.

At the same time, global infrastructure is increasingly integrated, international borders are porous, and nation-states have less ability to control the impact of global developments on domestic events. "National security" is less demanding in traditional ways but more demanding in defending against unfamiliar challenges to the U.S. territory and U.S. citizens and the functioning of vital global economic systems. High priorities include protecting critical information technology infrastructures, dealing with the prospect of WMD and non-WMD terrorism, international crime-fighting, and public health and ecological protection. Era B transformation is critical as U.S. forces adapt in order to deal with homeland security and other Achilles' heel–type challenges. Era A transformation is also important, but the priority efforts remain with longer-term transformation (that is, Era B). U.S. allies can handle the immediate security challenges they face, and the U.S. public's support for the defense of both the "old core" (the U.S. industrial base and U.S. territory) and the "new core" (global markets and information systems) remains strong.

BUILDING PROVISIONAL CONSTRUCTS BY RATING FORCE POSTURES AND CAPABILITY PACKAGES

The next step is to build *provisional constructs* by examining how the different approaches found in the constructs compare given the relative importance of the various force postures and special capability packages. By rating each posture and package as "very important," "important," or "less important," we form the provisional constructs. (These constructs are considered "provisional" because they do not account for the impact of the future security environment or fiscal constraints.) The posture and capabilities ratings for the constructs were derived by combining, in a pretty straightforward way, the ratings of the postures and capabilities for the constituent strategic themes, which were presented in Chapter Three.

The relative importance of the postures and capabilities for each provisional construct are summarized in Table 4.1.

For cases in which the rankings for the constituent themes of a construct differed, we tended to give extra weight to the theme that called for greater capability. That is, combining a "very important" rating with an "important" rating resulted in a "very important" rating. For example, the Expeditionary Forces posture is rated "very important" for the Countering Rogues theme and "important" for the Preparing for China theme (see Chapter Three). When these themes are combined for the Focus on Key Responsibilities construct, the new construct's rating for the Expeditionary Forces posture becomes "very important" (see Table 4.1).

Along the same lines, there were two instances in which a construct combined two significantly divergent assessments—"very important" and "less important." In those cases, we also biased the rating for the provisional construct upward. For example, the Missile Defense capability package is rated "very important" for the Protecting the Homeland theme and "less important" for the Countering New Dangers theme. When these themes are combined for the Protecting an Essential Core construct, the new construct's rating for the Expeditionary Forces posture becomes "very important." These choices were judgment calls, but displaying them in the provisional constructs permits their pros and cons to be debated.

Table 4.1

Posture and Capability Ratings for the Provisional Constructs

	Focus on Key Responsibilities	U.S. Multilateral Leadership	Protecting an Essential Core
Force Postures			
Traditionally Configured Combat Forces	Important	Important	Less Important
Expeditionary Forces	Very Important	Very Important	Very Important
Forces-After-Next Focus	Very Important	Less Important	Very Important
Special Capability Packages			
Stability Operations	Important	Very Important	Less Important
Missile Defense	Very Important	Less Important	Very Important
Countering WMD	Very Important	Important	Very Important
Countering Transnational Threats	Important	Important	Very Important
Information Operations	Very Important	Very Important	Very Important
Environment Shaping	Very Important	Very Important	Important
Nontraditional Missions	Less Important	Very Important	Less Important

To the extent that there is a strategic rationale for the upward bias, it probably would be prudent and conservative defense planning. It is safer to have more capability when it is needed than to risk winding up with less than what is required for a specific conflict. But the upward bias is present, and pushing up the requirements also pushes up the budget amounts.

The Focus on Key Responsibilities Provisional Construct

Both an Expeditionary Forces and a Forces-After-Next Focus posture are very important in this construct. The need for rapid deployability and lethality to defeat rogues and project force into Asia accounts for the importance of the Expeditionary Forces posture, while the necessity of preparing for a near peer drives the importance of the Forces-After-Next Focus posture. An Expeditionary Forces posture may have a slightly higher priority because it ranked "important," at least, for both the constituent themes of Preparing for China and Countering Rogues (whereas a Forces-After-Next Focus posture is "very important" for the first theme but "less important" for the second). A Traditionally Configured Combat Forces posture is nevertheless important to this construct because of the need for significant continued military presence as U.S. forces transition to an Expeditionary Forces posture.

In terms of special capability packages, Missile Defense, Information Operations, Countering WMD, and Environment Shaping are rated "very important." These capabilities help to defend U.S. territory and forces from missile or WMD attacks and from attacks on information systems; they also influence U.S. partners or potential adversaries and stabilize an area after a change in regimes in a defeated rogue state. Countering Transnational Threats is important in dealing with rogue-sponsored terrorism and illegal drug trade. Nontraditional Missions, by comparison, is a less important capability.

The U.S. Multilateral Leadership Provisional Construct

An Expeditionary Forces posture is the most useful in this construct because it facilitates the conduct of multiple SSCs and humanitarian relief efforts. The Traditionally Configured Combat Forces posture also is important as more expeditionary units are being developed, while the Forces-After-Next Focus is the least important posture for the expected challenges in this construct.

Environment Shaping, Information Operations, Stability Operations, and Nontraditional Missions are very important because of the crucial role these capability packages play in influencing the security environment and in coping with the mostly lower-end contingencies that are expected. Countering WMD and Countering Transnational Threats are important capabilities in instances in which potential U.S. adversaries attempt to employ anti-access strategies. Given the positive nature of the overall environment, capabilities such as Missile Defense are less important.

The Protecting an Essential Core Provisional Construct

In this construct, both an Expeditionary Forces and a Forces-After-Next Focus posture are very important because they focus on both the near-term and longer-term challenges in protecting the U.S. territory and its population. Traditionally Configured Combat Forces, by comparison, is a much less important posture.

Countering WMD, Countering Transnational Threats, Information Operations, and Missile Defense all require greater emphasis than do the other capabilities for this construct. They work to protect U.S. territory, the nation's information systems, the forces abroad, and U.S. allies from various forms of attack. Environment Shaping needs continued emphasis because it helps the United States develop international partnerships to defeat attacks against the country and its allies that are planned overseas. With the focus on defending the homeland, Stability Operations and Nontraditional Missions are less-important capabilities.

ASSESSING THE PROVISIONAL CONSTRUCTS

The provisional constructs turned out to be pretty consistent. The respective assessments for each of the constituent themes were generally the same or very similar. In other words, the pairs of themes used in each construct depended on quite similar capability sets. In the building of the provisional constructs, there were only two instances in which a "very important" rating was combined with a "less important" rating. These sorts of divergent ratings do not necessarily imply that a particular construct is "bad" or that choosing it would be unwise. It does give an indication, however, of the critical tradeoffs or choices that are implied in the building of a construct.

As mentioned earlier, these constructs are provisional because they do not account for the impact of the future security environment or fiscal constraints. The next step, therefore, is to refine these constructs based on their potential vulnerabilities, as identified in a review of the future security environment.

TESTING THE CONSTRUCTS AGAINST THE FUTURE SECURITY ENVIRONMENT

American military strategy should be based on the country's values and interests—that is, what the United States stands for in the world—but those values and interests should also be tempered by assessments of what the future security environment will require, permit, or facilitate. There are a number of ways to frame the future security environment, which would in turn test strategies in often-distinct ways.[1]

USING DRIVERS, NOT POINT PREDICTIONS OR SCENARIOS, AS METRICS

One way to assess the future security environment is to simply make best guesses, or point predictions, about key dimensions of the future. This approach is clear and simple, and it can be provocative. However, any point prediction is, by definition, almost sure to be wrong. Analytically, a best guess—that is, the "most likely" picture of the future—may only be 2-percent likely to happen, or only a fraction more likely to happen than 50 other eventualities, each of which might be judged to have only a 1-percent likelihood of becoming true. Point predictions, in that context, give far too much emphasis to one eventuality and far too little to the 50 others.

Building scenarios is another way of framing the future. However, when scenarios are used badly, they can confuse rather than clarify

---

[1] See, for instance, Schwartz (1991), Ascher and Overholt (1983), and Mintzberg (1994).

the issue. The temptation exists to build broad scenarios that, in effect, attempt to cover every possible outcome. But the point of using scenarios is to do precisely the opposite—create a number of possible pictures of the future not because any of them will necessarily happen but because they will provoke thought about future directions.

Perhaps a better technique is to examine several excursions derived from a "best guess" judgment that address not the most likely alternatives but rather those that would have the biggest impact on strategy. This technique, like the technique involving scenarios, is not designed to predict the future but to compel thought about what would have to happen to make an excursion become true. Signposts might be used as part of this approach to indicate that the excursion was becoming more likely to happen. When used well, both the scenario and the excursion technique can certainly be thought provoking. Nevertheless, they have the defect of multiplying complexity and can easily make the analysis unwieldy.

Our framework approach, by comparison, analyzes the future security environment by seeking to identify determinants, or "drivers," that will bear on future U.S. and allied military operations. Drivers are not meant to represent either underlying causes or symptoms of problems in the security environment. Rather, they are intended to be "mid-level" constructions that are general enough in their design to have some effect across almost all possible future security environments, but specific enough to allow the future-environment analysis to identify the effect in particular.

The use of the term "drivers" and the effort to identify them are purposeful. The ten drivers represent a compromise between analytic richness and manageability. There is nothing sacred about the list of drivers; it is subjective and could be lengthened or shortened. The drivers are intended to be separable for purposes of testing the constructs, but they are not mutually independent.[2]

---

[2]A similar approach to examining the future security environment is found in the concluding chapter of *Strategic Assessment: Engaging Power for Peace* (1998) pp. 274–277.

CATEGORIZING THE TEN DRIVERS

Each driver is expressed as a positive assumption:[3]

- Such-and-such *will* occur.

- And that occurrence would, on balance, be *good* for the United States if the driver turned out as stated.

Phrasing the drivers as positive assumptions comes into play later in the framework-development process when the strategic themes are tested against the drivers.

The ten posited drivers are divided into three broad categories as defined by the following questions:[4]

- How will future political and economic developments be seen within a global context?

- How much capacity will the United States have?

- What drives the security threats that the United States may face?

Thus stated, the drivers within each category are as follows:

Drivers Within a Global Context

- **Positive globalization will continue.** The positive side of globalization is the open global economy and the opportunities for economic growth it presents, along with the incentives that economic interchange implies for at least the core industrial nations, including the United States, to cooperate with each other. This positive side of globalization also includes the incentives that nations now outside the core have to shape their politics and their economic strategies in order to become part of the global economy.[5]

---

[3]This method is very much akin to that found in Dewar et al. (1993).

[4]For parallel listings, see the U.S. Commission on National Security/21st Century (1999) and National Intelligence Council (2001).

[5]There is a vast literature and long debate on whether economic interdependence or the spread of democracy will lead to a more peaceful world. So-called realists argue

- **Negative globalization will be limited.** Because the negative aspects of globalization—crime, drug dealing, and illegal weapons trading—flow across borders as readily as the positive aspects, such as economic growth, that flow of "bads" is the primary downside of globalization. Another negative side of globalization, from the U.S. perspective, is that economic growth and the diffusion of technology will upset existing power balances, in particular, leading to a rise of power in Asia. A third negative side consists of the constraints on U.S. policy that result when the United States acquires broad interests in economic interchange with a particular nation. For instance, the United States could not retain economic sanctions against India for long after India's 1998 nuclear tests and, despite the acrimonious debate in Congress, granting permanent normal trading relations with China in 2000 was all but a foregone conclusion.[6] A final negative aspect of globalization may be in the form of extreme distributional problems. The upper classes in Western states generally will do well under globalization, but the lower classes may be hurt significantly by the exporting of industries to places where labor is cheap.

- **Transnational trends, such as increased migration or environmental degradation, will not affect military operations or definitions of security.** These trends are *not* the result of a willful adversary's intent to do the United States harm but rather are the result of cumulative actions of many individuals undertaken for other reasons. For instance, those who burn the Amazon rain forest do so *not* with the intent of increasing global warming— they do so to survive. In that sense, if such trends become threatening to the United States, they are essentially "threats without threateners."[7]

---

that neither of them will; the world will remain, in Kenneth Waltz's word, "anarchic," in which security competition continues and war sometimes ensues (Waltz, 1979). In contrast, the "liberal" approach focuses not on states but on individuals, and it locates the determinants of state behavior more in its internal institutions than in the imperatives of the international system. A more optimistic view is that political and economic change can lead to a more peaceful world. See, for instance, Fukuyama (1992) and Doyle (1997).

[6]For a detailed discussion of the India case, see Treverton (2000).

[7]This language is from Treverton (1999), pp. 39–56. In fact, "threats" might be conceived across a continuum with, say, determined terrorists at one end, those who burn

Drivers Related to U.S. Capacity

- **The United States will be rich and technologically advantaged relative to both friends and foes.** The current U.S. technological advantage is unusually high, but the country can continue to maintain a competitive edge with the right type of investments, both capital investments and investments in its relationships with allies and partners.

- **The United States will have domestic support for considerable defense spending.** Defense spending has declined since the end of the Cold War, but domestic support for considerable defense expenditures is still strong. This support will remain significant, even if defense budgets are not likely to approach the pre-1989 levels.

- **The United States will have domestic support for substantial engagement.** The American public will continue to recognize the importance of being engaged in the world through the use of combined military exercises, military-to-military exchanges, and other activities.

- **The United States will have rich and strong allies.** U.S. allies' military capacity and economic success will continue to grow in ways that coincide with U.S. interests.

Drivers Related to Threats Against the United States and Its Allies

- **Large states, especially China, but also Russia and India, will make successful transitions toward pluralistic political systems and market economics.** Free trade will further strengthen these transitions and the democratic core of nation-states will continue to enlarge.

- **Attacks on information systems and WMD attacks will remain isolated and/or contained.** It has become conventional wisdom, and appropriately so, that would-be U.S. adversaries, including

---

rain forests at the other end, and criminals and drug traffickers somewhere in the middle. Some individuals do not explicitly intend to harm the United States; they only want to get rich and the harm they inflict on society is an incidental by-product.

foreign states, would be foolish to take on the United States in an area where it is strong—conventional military battle. Therefore, these would-be adversaries will pursue *asymmetric* strategies, looking for points of weakness or vulnerability in U.S. defenses. WMD attacks and perhaps attacks on information systems, for example, present attractive ways to circumvent U.S. strengths and engage in conflict on terms that are favorable to the U.S. adversary.[8]

- **States may fail, but the effects of their failures will remain localized.** That is, as states crumble under the weight of their own corruption, inefficiency, and ethnic rivalry, they may spew violent action or create large numbers of emigrants. But in this positive formulation, those negative effects will be contained mostly in the states' immediate regions.[9]

ASSUMPTIONS INHERENT IN THE STRATEGIC THEMES

In this examination of future drivers, it is more analytically satisfying to work at the building-block level with the strategic themes (described in Chapter Two) than at the more-aggregated level of constructs (see Chapter Four). Because single themes have a sharper emphasis than constructs that encompass more than one theme, they reflect distinct biases about the future. The Ambitious Shaping theme, for example, is boldly optimistic, whereas the Countering Rogues theme, on the other hand, is more profoundly pessimistic. For each strategic theme, we asked the following questions:

- What assumptions about each driver are inherent in each theme?

- How important is each assumption?

- Which assumptions are most vulnerable to *not* turning out as stated?

---

[8]For one formulation for countering asymmetric threats, see Treverton and Bennett (1997). For early works on information threats as asymmetric threats, see Molander et al. (1996) and Arquilla and Ronfeldt (1997).

[9]Robert D. Kaplan's evocative article (Kaplan, 1994) contributed to the attention paid to failed states, and perhaps also to a misunderstanding of them by seeming to lump together their different causes.

This process may seem more complicated than it really is. Looking at the assumptions inherent in the themes should make the process clearer.

Assumptions Inherent in Ambitious Shaping

This theme encompasses a number of strong and positive assumptions about the future security environment. The positive facets of globalization will continue to be strong. The democratic core will not fracture, and increased economic interchange will provide more reasons for states to cooperate, not more opportunities for argument and conflict. The U.S. public will support an expansive engagement with both allies and transition states. Transition states, although not likely to become stable democratic partners any time soon, have good prospects of continuing to move in that direction. And U.S. allies become real partners. This theme is also based on strong assumptions that neither the failure of states nor, especially, threats to information systems and WMD threats will redirect the U.S. defense agenda.

Among the assumptions for the Ambitious Shaping theme, four are vulnerable to not happening as anticipated (see Figure 5.1). These assumptions are vulnerable because if they do not turn out as stated, they could endanger or cast doubt on the viability or wisdom of the entire theme. For example, what if the transition states falter in their transitions? Or what if the U.S. public no longer continues to support an ambitious engagement of U.S. forces given the absence of a visible enemy? And what about the U.S. allies? Can they be counted on to be engaged as ever-closer partners and take part in reaching out to transition states? Or suppose globalization begins to fracture, resulting in nationalist economic policies muting cooperation among nations, declining growth, and rising trade barriers. In addition, although the assumptions can be analyzed independently of one another, they are nevertheless interrelated. If, for example, states begin to falter in their transition to becoming stable democratic partners, the U.S. public might become less supportive of engagement.

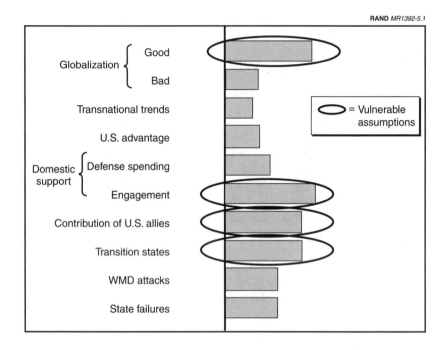

Figure 5.1—Assumptions Inherent in the Ambitious Shaping Theme

In Figure 5.1, the length of a bar signifies the strength of an assumption that a driver will turn out as expected. For example, the Ambitious Shaping theme is very bullish on the positive impact of globalization, domestic support for engagement, the ability of U.S. allies to contribute to world security, and the fate of transition states. The theme is less sanguine about, but nevertheless strong on, the limited negative impact of globalization, transnational trends, continued U.S. military advantage, domestic support for defense spending, the prospects for preventing WMD attacks, and the limited impact of state failures.

If, given the Ambitious Shaping theme, a driver is expected to "break" (that is, not come true), the bar for that driver would appear to the left of the vertical line in Figure 5.1. The same holds true for Figures 5.2 through 5.6, in which gray bars appear to the right of the vertical line, indicating that those drivers *are not* expected to break, and black bars appear to the left of the line, indicating that those drivers *are* expected to break.

Assumptions Inherent in Countering Rogues

The Countering Rogues theme anticipates that the positive aspects of globalization will continue but that its underside will also become apparent—for example, as the spread of technology empowers rogues as well as the United States and its allies. Figure 5.2 illustrates the assumptions for this theme. The Countering Rogues theme also has the expectation that the U.S. military advantage and domestic support for defense and engagement will remain strong. More negatively, the theme anticipates that some state failures will adversely, but not significantly, impact regional stability; a few transition states will not succeed, though with little effect on the geopolitical situation; and WMD attacks will likely happen, but they should build support for U.S. policies.

RAND *MR1392-5.2*

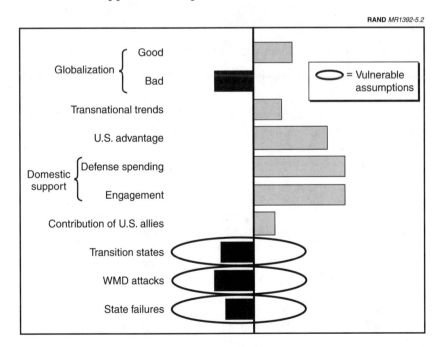

Figure 5.2—Assumptions Inherent in the Countering Rogues Theme

Three drivers are vulnerable to "breaking." Although the theme assumes that each of these three drivers will break (that is, not turn out to be a positively stated driver), they could turn out even worse than expected. Anticipated failures of some transition states, for example, could produce major rogues. Catastrophic WMD attacks could destroy U.S. resolve. Multiple state failures could significantly undermine stability in key regions.

Assumptions Inherent in Protecting the Homeland

Concentration on the defense of U.S. territory makes the assumptions for this theme quite different from the assumptions for the other themes. This theme has the expectation that domestic support for defense will be extremely strong because the homeland is under threat. The theme does not expect much in the way of contributions from allies, but it does assume that U.S. technological advantages will continue. It is pessimistic about future state failures, the future of transition states, and, especially, the possibility of WMD attacks (see Figure 5.3).

The most vulnerable assumptions for the Protecting the Homeland theme are the continued U.S. military advantage and the fate of major transition states. If a United States that is less reliant on allies and more inwardly focused loses its comparative technological advantage, or if a major state such as Russia (as opposed to a smaller transition state such as the Ukraine) fails and becomes hostile, this theme will be in danger.

Assumptions Inherent in Countering New Dangers

The Countering New Dangers theme has the expectation that the underside of globalization will significantly impact the future security environment. The flow of crime, people, pollutants, and disease as a result of the negative aspects of globalization will affect military operations and definitions of security. States are expected to fail and the "bads" from their collapse will spill over to the United States and the rest of the world. WMD threats, however, are not expected to be significant. Allied contributions and cooperation and domestic support for engagement are expected to be critical in this struggle against new dangers (see Figure 5.4).

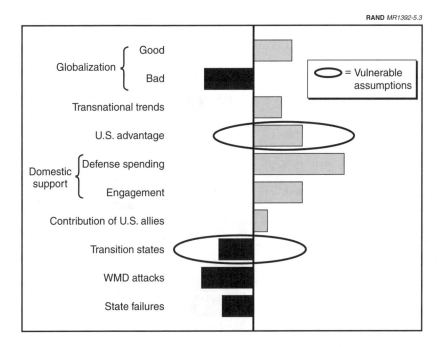

RAND *MR1392-5.3*

Figure 5.3—Assumptions Inherent in the Protecting the Homeland Theme

Three of the Protecting the Homeland assumptions are particularly vulnerable. If support for U.S. military shaping activities abates or U.S. allies prove to be disappointing in their level of support, countering transnational threats could become exceedingly difficult. Similarly, if transnational groups are able to conduct several major WMD attacks, the theme could be undermined.

Assumptions Inherent in Preparing for China

The Preparing for China theme presents a less optimistic view of the future than do the other themes. This theme anticipates that the bad effects of globalization will have a significant impact on the future security environment, some transition states will not succeed, and WMD attacks will happen. On the positive side, this theme carries with it the expectation that the U.S. military and economic advantage over China and over other transition states continues, domestic

RAND *MR1392-5.4*

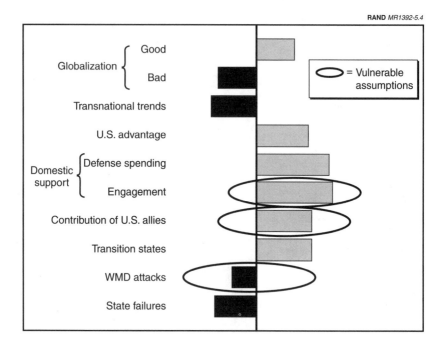

Figure 5.4—Assumptions Inherent in the Countering New Dangers Theme

support for defense remains strong because of the threat of possible Chinese power, but also, somewhat paradoxically, U.S. economic interests in China work to maintain domestic support for engagement. The impact of the good effects of globalization is not expected to be extensive because those positive effects will tend to disperse power among a number of states. More critical to the theme, U.S. allies in Europe and Asia are not expected to be strong, but we expect them to handle their own security problems.

There are two principal vulnerabilities in this theme (see Figure 5.5). First, the theme relies on continued U.S. domestic support for engagement with China even as the United States also prepares for the possibility of confronting China as a military adversary. That would imply walking a fine line, perhaps too fine. As China inevitably is cast as a potential enemy, domestic support for engaging China would erode. Second, this theme also assumes that allies can be relied on to handle their own security problems, but what if allies prove

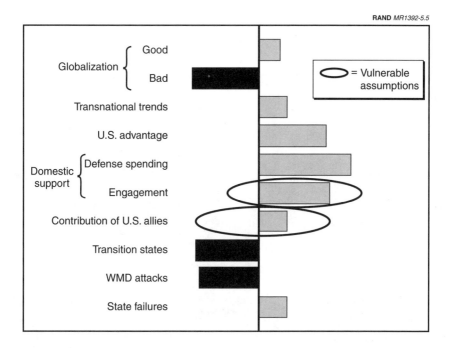

Figure 5.5—Assumptions Inherent in the Preparing for China Theme

to be disappointing in their level of support? This theme is undermined in either of these two cases.

Assumptions Inherent in Policing Instability

In this theme, the bad aspects of globalization are expected to lead to
instability in some areas, perhaps undermining key states located in
critical regions. Transnational threats combine with traditional military ones. However, WMD threats are not expected to be a major
problem. Domestic and allied support for engagement and military
action is critical for success (see Figure 5.6).

There are three vulnerable assumptions for the Policing Instability
theme. If repeated SSCs are unsuccessful and cause large numbers of
U.S. casualties, domestic support for engagement may evaporate.
Similarly, the inability or unwillingness of allies to provide military

RAND MR1392-5.6

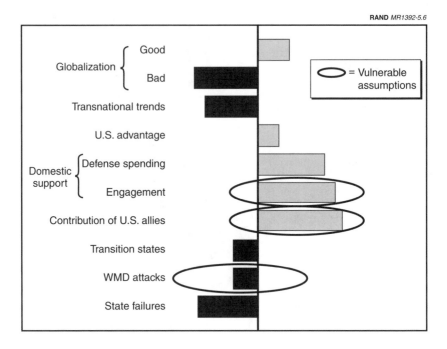

Figure 5.6—Assumptions Inherent in the Policing Instability Theme

and political support, or the introduction of WMD threats or attacks into this low-end environment, could undermine this theme.

VULNERABLE ASSUMPTIONS

As noted earlier, if certain assumptions do not turn out as stated, the negative outcomes could endanger or cast doubt on the viability or wisdom of the respective theme. The judgments regarding the assumptions and their vulnerabilities are necessarily subjective, but they point out key areas where the themes are susceptible to being undermined. In summarizing the analysis in the previous sections, Table 5.1 presents the vulnerable assumptions across all the themes.

As shown in Table 5.1, the vulnerable assumptions are largely clustered within the following drivers: domestic support for engagement, support from U.S. allies, future prospects for transition states, and

Table 5.1

Vulnerable Assumptions Across the Themes

Theme	Good Globalization	Bad Globalization	Transnational Threats	U.S. Technological Advantage	Domestic Support for Defense	Domestic Support for Engagement	U.S. Allies	Transition States	WMD Attacks, Including Attacks to Information Operations	State Failure
Ambitious Shaping	X					X	X	X		
Countering Rogues								X	X	X
Protecting the Homeland				X				X		
Countering New Dangers						X	X		X	
Preparing for China						X	X			
Policing Instability						X	X		X	

the magnitude of the threat of WMD attacks. Because the drivers are expressed in positive terms, this clustering pattern would suggest the following for the six themes:

- U.S. domestic support for engagement abroad may be weaker than what the themes would suggest.
- Allies may be less supportive than anticipated.
- Prospects for transition states may be less rosy than one would hope.
- Attacks to information systems and WMD threats and attacks may be much more of a problem than expected.

Chapter Six

REFINING THE CONSTRUCTS

The last stage in building the strategic framework is refining the provisional constructs that were presented in Chapter Four to take into account the tests against the future security environment that were presented in Chapter Five. This refinement will turn the provisional constructs into *portfolios* of decisionmaking options that imply resource choices.

The first step in the transition from provisional constructs to illustrative portfolios is made by changing the terms of the ratings for each force posture and special capability package. In the provisional constructs, the force postures and special capability packages were rated in terms of their relative strategic importance for each construct (see Table 4.1). In the illustrative portfolios, those ratings become terms of budgetary priority. Specifically, a posture or capability that is "very important" becomes one in which to "invest" (that is, increase the investment in that posture or capability if desired and if the investment proves to be fruitful); a posture or capability that is "important" becomes one to "maintain" (that is, recapitalize and modernize the posture or capability as necessary and fund related operations); and a "less important" posture or capability becomes one to "divest" (that is, consider reducing the investment in that posture or capability or eliminate the investment in it altogether).

The next step in the transition from provisional constructs to illustrative portfolios is to identify possible hedges for each construct based on the constructs' respective vulnerabilities noted in the future security environment analysis.

IDENTIFYING POSSIBLE HEDGES AGAINST VULNERABILITIES

The tests against the future security environment identified various vulnerable assumptions among the drivers of each theme. Aggregating to the level of constructs, the vulnerabilities translate from the constituent themes to their respective constructs (for example, the vulnerabilities for the Countering Rogues and Preparing for China themes become the vulnerabilities for the Focus on Key Responsibilities construct). Those vulnerable assumptions, which endanger the viability of an entire construct if they do not turn out as expected, are natural places to look for hedging opportunities. The following sections describe possible refinements to the constructs.

Refining the Focus on Key Responsibilities Construct

The Focus on Key Responsibilities construct implies a defense program that invests heavily in systems and platforms to exploit both Era A and Era B RMAs (see Chapter Four). Given that few divestments are identified, this likely means a significant increase in the DoD topline.

After examining the future security environment, several vulnerabilities in this construct become apparent. What if, for example, other problems outside of MTWs become important to U.S. interests? Similarly, what if a major transition state, such as Russia, becomes confrontational in the Balkans and the European allies are not able to deter the aggression without U.S. assistance? One possible hedge for this construct would be to maintain some capacity for nontraditional missions such as humanitarian assistance. The United States could provide food aid or disaster assistance to help keep Russia from failing and turning hostile.

Figure 6.1 illustrates how the Focus on Key Responsibilities construct might be refined given the implications of the construct, the vulnerabilities in the construct, and possible hedging options.

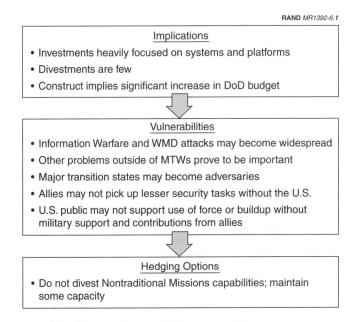

RAND *MR1392-6.1*

Figure 6.1—Possible Hedging Options for the Focus on
Key Responsibilities Construct

Refining the U.S. Multilateral Leadership Construct

In the U.S. Multilateral Leadership construct, the vulnerabilities are a
combination of those in the Ambitious Shaping and Policing Instability themes. Globalization's "bads" might outpace the good effects;
attacks on information systems and WMD attacks might become
major threats; major transition states might falter in their transformations, and even become adversaries; allies may disappoint the
United States in their lack of willingness or ability to partner with the
United States in defense activities; and domestic support could decline, especially if operations lead to U.S. casualties in what seem to
be increasingly dubious ventures.

These vulnerabilities could even serve to reinforce one another. For
example, a disappointing level of support from U.S. allies could contribute to eroding domestic support. The options for hedging against
these vulnerabilities might take the form of policy. If, for instance, al-

lies were reluctant to become involved in a wide range of joint military operations, diplomacy could exhort them to reconsider, or purely economic assistance might make it easier for them to act. If U.S. domestic support for engagement softened, the hedge might partly consist of more and better public arguments by U.S. leaders on the importance of engagement.

One possible hedge against the possibility of a failed major transition state would be to maintain—and not divest—a Forces-After-Next Focus force posture. By continuing R&D on Era B RMA efforts, the DoD can maintain some ability to change course if future developments do not work as planned. In terms of the capability portfolio, though, the hedges would focus on the Missile Defense capability, which was originally considered less important in the provisional Focus on Key Responsibilities construct. Missile defense was regarded to be unnecessary because the threats were judged to be deterred and limited, and was regarded to be unwise because missile defense connotes a "fortress America" to allies and other would-be coalition partners, just the opposite of the cooperative spirit at the heart of this construct. However, hedging against threats to information systems and WMD threats, and against the possibility that transition states might become adversaries, would move Missile Defense from being categorized as "less important" to being categorized as "important." As a result, R&D efforts on Missile Defense might continue. To be sure, the hedges carry costs, both monetary and, perhaps, in diverting capacity and distracting would-be allies.

Figure 6.2 illustrates how the U.S. Multilateral Leadership construct might be refined.

Refining the Protecting an Essential Core Construct

The Protecting an Essential Core construct is very focused on protecting U.S. territory while conducting a radical transformation of military forces to meet the challenges of the coming decades. As initially constructed, it divests Traditionally Configured Combat Forces, Stability Operations, and Nontraditional Missions.

But what if, for example, the U.S. technological advantage rapidly dissipates and a major transition state, such as China, becomes an adversary much sooner than expected? What if U.S. allies are unable

Implications
• Investments mostly in expeditionary forces and lower-end capabilities • Divestments centered more on systems and high-end capabilities • Current DoD topline would likely be sufficient

Vulnerabilities
• "Bads" of globalization may outpace "goods" • Information warfare and WMD attacks may become major threats • Major transition states may become adversaries • Allies may disappoint in their willingness or ability to partner with U.S. • Domestic support could decline with casualties

Hedging Options
• Do not divest Forces-After-Next Focus; continue R&D on Era B RMA • Do not suspend Missile Defense work; maintain R&D efforts

Figure 6.2—Possible Hedging Options for the U.S. Multilateral Leadership Construct

to contribute to the protection and maintenance of the global economic system and, therefore, the positive aspects of globalization begin to diminish over time? Problems in the international political and economic environment could lead to a decline in U.S. domestic support for engagement activities, further destabilizing U.S. security.

To hedge against these and other possibilities, the United States could maintain traditionally configured forces in the near term. This measure would allow the DoD to respond to immediate threats while it is developing and fielding an Era A transformation force. To shore up the political and economic situations in key regions, the DoD could maintain some capacity to conduct stability operations. In addition to the security this hedging would provide, it would also help to maintain relationships with both allies and critical transition states.

Figure 6.3 illustrates how the Protecting an Essential Core construct might be refined.

BUILDING ILLUSTRATIVE PORTFOLIOS

At this point in the development of the strategic framework, we can build refined constructs or, more appropriately, *portfolios.* The portfolios identify key strategic points of emphasis in terms of the force postures and special capability packages.

Table 6.1 summarizes the refined portfolios for each construct, and also indicates a few hedges that are possible, but not necessary, refinements to the constructs (again, see Table 4.1 for comparison).

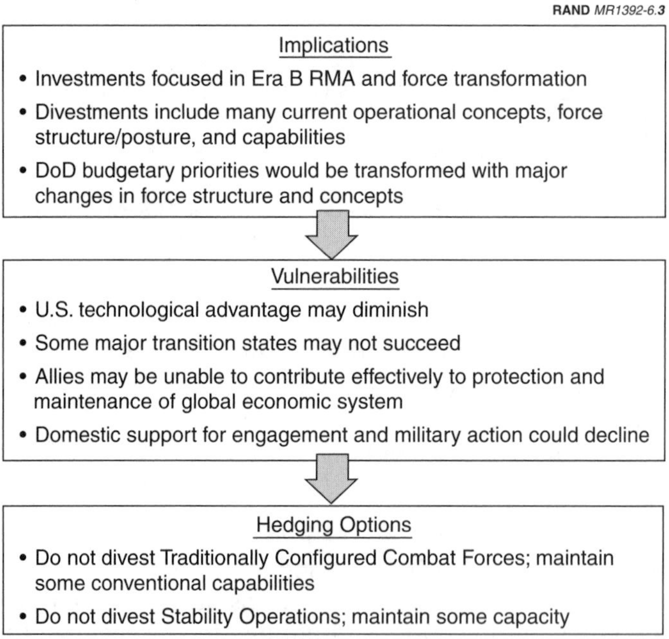

RAND MR1392-6.3

Implications
- Investments focused in Era B RMA and force transformation
- Divestments include many current operational concepts, force structure/posture, and capabilities
- DoD budgetary priorities would be transformed with major changes in force structure and concepts

Vulnerabilities
- U.S. technological advantage may diminish
- Some major transition states may not succeed
- Allies may be unable to contribute effectively to protection and maintenance of global economic system
- Domestic support for engagement and military action could decline

Hedging Options
- Do not divest Traditionally Configured Combat Forces; maintain some conventional capabilities
- Do not divest Stability Operations; maintain some capacity

Figure 6.3—Possible Hedging Options for the Protecting an Essential Core Construct

Table 6.1 indicates three "hedged" strategic choices—that is, choices that were modified in response to vulnerabilities identified in the future security environment. Under U.S. Multilateral Leadership, for example, Missile Defense would have been categorized under "divest" had it not been hedged to a "maintain" status based on the tests against the future security environment. Although we have identified several potential hedges, not all of them are necessary or prudent. We can, for example, still significantly cut traditionally configured forces while maintaining some capability in the near term because some expeditionary forces already exist.

We can now also begin to draw out the resource implications of making certain strategic choices. Deciding to pursue the Protecting an Essential Core construct, for example, will lead to major changes

Table 6.1

Illustrative Portfolios of Key Decisionmaking Options

	Focus on Key Responsibilities	U.S. Multilateral Leadership	Protecting an Essential Core
Force Postures			
Traditionally Configured Combat Forces	Maintain	Maintain	Divest
Expeditionary Forces	Invest	Invest	Invest
Forces-After-Next Focus	Invest	Maintain[a]	Invest
Special Capability Packages			
Stability Operations	Maintain	Invest	Maintain[a]
Missile Defense	Invest	Maintain[a]	Invest
Countering WMD	Invest	Maintain	Invest
Countering Transnational Threats	Maintain	Maintain	Invest
Information Operations	Invest	Invest	Invest
Environment Shaping	Invest	Invest	Maintain
Nontraditional Missions	Divest	Invest	Divest

[a]Hedged strategic choices modified in response to identified vulnerabilities in the future security environment.

in the structure and posture of U.S. military forces. In comparison, such a radical transformation is not the top priority in the Focus on Key Responsibilities construct and is not a priority at all in the U.S. Multilateral Leadership construct. These sorts of resource implications resound throughout the portfolios.

Chapter Seven

APPLYING THE FRAMEWORK

The complete strategic framework, while seemingly complicated, can be a powerful decisionmaking tool for prioritizing various needs. Looking across the portfolios within the framework (shown in Figure 7.1) helps to clearly identify key strategic decisions that must be made:

- Which core postures and capability packages are necessary in almost every case, regardless of which strategy is chosen?

- Which core postures and capability packages are less necessary in almost every case, regardless of which strategy is chosen?

- Where do strategic choices—in terms of their emphasis and in terms of resources—need to be made?

The core forces and capabilities are those force postures and special capability packages that all three portfolios will either invest in or maintain. Thus, they form a nucleus of key attributes that are important to decisionmakers regardless of the chosen defense strategy. The key decisions and tradeoffs are those that entail expanding from the core forces and capabilities in order to encompass one or another illustrative portfolio. Moving toward the Protecting an Essential Core portfolio, for example, makes a Forces-After-Next Focus the top priority and suggests divesting capacity for Traditionally Configured Combat Forces and Nontraditional Missions. Moving toward the U.S. Multilateral Leadership portfolio, on the other hand, reverses those priorities.

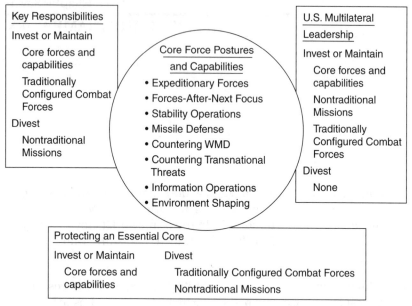

Figure 7.1—Using the Framework to Identify Strategic Choices

There is also significant room for differentiation within the core forces and capabilities. Although the core covers two of the three force postures and six of the seven special capability packages, there are differences in "invest" versus "maintain" among the three portfolios. So, although the three portfolios will have certain postures and packages in common, there will be potentially significant differences in emphasis within this core set. Moreover, while these three portfolios happen to have a relatively high degree of complementarity, other constructs might imply a different and less broad set of common postures and capabilities.

The framework is readily adaptable to building other strategies. Different themes can be articulated and themes can be mixed and matched to build constructs other than those we use in this report to illustrate how the framework can be applied. The framework also allows changes in assessments of the future security environment to result in different strategic choices.

Spelling out force postures and capability packages gives clarity to the inherent—but not always readily visible—resource implications of strategic choices and tradeoffs. In that sense, the framework provides a mechanism for connecting the defense strategy to programmatic choices and debating the pros and cons of those choices.

BIBLIOGRAPHY

1998 Strategic Assessment: Engaging Power for Peace, Washington, D.C.: National Defense University Press, 1998.

Arquilla, John, and David Rodfeldt, *In Athena's Camp: Preparing for Conflict in the Information Age*, Santa Monica, Calif.: RAND, MR-880-OSD/RC, 1997.

Ascher, William, and William H. Overholt, *Strategic Planning and Forecasting: Political Risk and Economic Opportunity*, New York: John Wiley & Sons, 1983.

Betts, Richard K., "Is Strategy an Illusion?" *International Security*, Vol. 25, No. 2, Fall 2000, pp. 5–50.

Carter, Ashton B., "Adapting US Defence to Future Needs," *Survival*, Vol. 41, No. 4, Winter 1999–2000), pp. 101–123.

_____, "Keeping America's Military Edge," *Foreign Affairs*, Vol. 80, No. 1, January/February 2001, pp. 90–105.

Cohen, William S., *Annual Report to the President and the Congress*, Washington, D.C., 2001. Available at http://www.dtic.mil/execsec/adr2001/ (last accessed December 27, 2001).

_____, *Report of the Quadrennial Defense Review*, U.S. Department of Defense, Washington, D.C., 1997. Available at http://www.defenselink.mil/pubs/qdr/ (last accessed January 3, 2002).

Davis, Paul K., ed., *New Challenges for Defense Planning: Rethinking How Much is Enough,* Santa Monica, Calif.: RAND, MR-400-RC, 1994.

Davis, Paul K., David Gompert, and Richard Kugler, *Adaptiveness in National Defense: The Basis of a New Framework,* Santa Monica, Calif.: RAND, IP-155, 1996.

Davis, Paul K., David Gompert, Richard J. Hillestad, and Stuart Johnson, *Transforming the Force: Suggestions for DoD Strategy,* Santa Monica, Calif.: RAND, IP-179, 1998.

Dewar, James A., et al., *Assumption-Based Planning: A Planning Tool for Very Uncertain Times,* Santa Monica, Calif.: RAND, MR-114A, 1993.

Doyle, Michael W., *Ways of War and Peace,* New York: W.W. Norton, 1997.

Farer, Tom. J., *Transnational Crime in the Americas,* New York: Routledge, 1999.

Flournoy, Michèle A., *Report of the National Defense University Quadrennial Defense Review 2001 Working Group,* Washington, D.C.: National Defense University Press, 2000.

Fukuyama, Francis, *The End of History and the Last Man,* New York: Free Press, 1992.

Gompert, David C., and Irving Lachow, *Transforming U.S. Forces: Lessons from the Wider Revolution,* Santa Monica, Calif.: RAND, IP-193, 2000.

Gouré, Daniel, and Jeffrey M. Ranney, *Averting the Defense Train Wreck in the New Millennium,* Center for Strategic and International Studies, Washington, D.C.: The CSIS Press, 1999.

Herz, John, *Political Realism and Political Idealism,* Chicago: The University of Chicago Press, 1951.

Hillestad, Richard J., and Paul K. Davis, *Resource Allocation for the New Defense Strategy: The DynaRank Decision-Support System,* Santa Monica, Calif.: RAND, MR-966-OSD, 1998.

Huntington, Samuel P., "The Lonely Superpower," *Foreign Affairs.* Vol. 78, No. 2, March/April 1999, p. 35.

Kaplan, Robert D., "The Coming Anarchy," *The Atlantic,* Vol. 273, No. 2, February 1994, pp. 44–76.

Kapstein, Ethan B., and Michael Mastanduno, eds., *Unipolar Politics,* New York: Columbia University Press, 1999.

Layne, Christopher, "Rethinking American Grand Strategy," *World Policy Journal,* Vol. 15, No. 2, Summer 1998, pp. 8–28.

_____, "The Unipolar Illusion: Why New Great Powers Will Rise," *International Security,* Vol. 17, No. 4, Spring 1993, pp. 5–51.

Macgregor, Douglas A., *Breaking the Phalanx: A New Design for Landpower in the 21st Century,* Westport, Conn.: Praeger, 1997.

Mintzberg, Henry, *The Rise and Fall of Strategic Planning,* New York: The Free Press, 1994.

Molander, Roger, Andrew Riddile, and Peter Wilson, *Strategic Information Warfare: A New Face of War,* Santa Monica, Calif.: RAND, MR-661-OSD, 1996.

National Defense Panel, *Transforming Defense: National Security in the 21st Century,* Arlington, Va., December 1997. Available at http://www.dtic.mil/ndp (last accessed December 27, 2001).

National Intelligence Council, *Global Trends 2015,* Washington, D.C.: Central Intelligence Agency, 2001.

Owens, William, *Lifting the Fog of War,* New York: Farrar, Straus, and Giroux, 2000.

Rice, Condoleezza, "Promoting the National Interest," *Foreign Affairs,* Vol. 79, No. 1, January/February 2000, p. 45–62.

Schwartz, Peter, *The Art of the Long View,* New York: Doubleday, 1991.

Schweller, Randall L., "Realism and the Present Great Power System: Growth and Positional Conflict Over Scarce Resources," in Ethan

B. Kapstein and Michael Mastanduno, eds., *Unipolar Politics,* New York: Columbia University Press, 1999.

Tedstrom, John E., and John G. McGinn, *Planning America's Security: Lessons from the National Defense Panel,* Santa Monica, Calif.: RAND, MR-1049-OSD, 1999.

Treverton, Gregory F., "Organized Crime, National Security, and the 'Market State,'" in Tom Farer, ed., *Transnational Crime in the Americas,* New York: Routledge, 1999, pp. 39–56.

_____, *Framing Compellent Strategies,* MR-1240-OSD, Santa Monica, Calif.: RAND, 2000.

Treverton, Gregory F., and Bruce Bennett, *Integrating Counterproliferation in Defense Planning,* Santa Monica, Calif.: RAND, IP-158, 1997.

U.S. Commission on National Security/21st Century, *New World Coming: American Security in the 21st Century, Major Themes and Implications,* Phase 1 Report, Washington, D.C.: September 15, 1999.

U.S. Congressional Budget Office, *Budgeting for Defense: Maintaining Today's Forces,* September 2000. Available at http://www.cbo.gov/showdoc.cfm?index=2398&sequence=0&from=1 (last accessed December 27, 2001).

_____, *Making Peace While Staying Ready for War: The Challenges of U.S. Military Participation in Peace Operations,* December 1999. Available at http://www.cbo.gov/showdoc.cfm?index=1809&sequence=0&from=1 (last accessed December 27, 2001).

_____, *Paying for Military Readiness and Upkeep: Trends in Operation and Maintenance Spending,* September 1997. Available at http://www.cbo.gov/showdoc.cfm?index=58&sequence=0&from=5 (last accessed December 27, 2001).

U.S. Department of Defense, *Quadrennial Defense Review Report,* Washington, D.C.: September 30, 2001. Available at http://www.defenselink.mil/pubs/qdr2001.pdf (last accessed December 27, 2001).

_____, Office of the Under Secretary of Defense (Comptroller), Defense Budget Materials, fiscal years 1999 to 2001 budget. Available at http://www.dtic.mil/comptroller (last accessed December 27, 2001).

_____, Office of the Under Secretary of Defense (Comptroller), *National Defense Budget Estimates for FY2000,* March 1999, pp. 108-111. Available at http://www.dtic.mil/comptroller/fy2000 budget/GREEN2000.pdf (last accessed January 2, 2002).

U.S. General Accounting Office, *Contingency Operations: Providing Critical Capabilities Poses Challenges,* GAO/NSIAD-00-164, July 2000. Available at http://www.gao.gov (last accessed December 27, 2001).

_____, *Military Operations: Impact of Operations Other Than War on the Services Varies,* GAO/NSIAD-99-69, May 1999. Available at http://www.gao.gov (last accessed December 27, 2001).

Walt, Stephen M., *The Origins of Alliances,* Ithaca, N.Y.: Cornell University Press, 1987.

Waltz, Kenneth, *Theory of International Politics,* Reading, Mass.: Addison Wesley, 1979.